Designing for Diversity

Designing for Diversity

*Developing inclusive and equitable
talent management processes*

Binna Kandola

KoganPage

First published in Great Britain and the United States in 2025 by Kogan Page Limited

2nd Floor, 45 Gee Street
London
EC1V 3RS
United Kingdom

8 W 38th Street, Suite 902
New York, NY 10018
USA

www.koganpage.com

Kogan Page books are printed on paper from sustainable forests.

ISBNs

Hardback   978 1 3986 1810 7
Paperback   978 1 3986 1808 4
Ebook   978 1 3986 1809 1

British Library Cataloguing-in-Publication Data

A CIP record for this book is available from the British Library.

Library of Congress Control Number

2024952408

Typeset by Integra Software Services, Pondicherry
Print production managed by Jellyfish
Printed and bound by CPI Group (UK) Ltd, Croydon, CR0 4YY

CONTENTS

1

Introduction

Talent management and the 'war for talent':
A way of maintaining the status quo

In Westminster Abbey, nestled among the tombs of kings, queens and other notable figures from British history, are the remains of James Rennell (1742–1830). Not as recognizable as others interred at the Abbey, including Jane Austen, Robert Burns, Charles Darwin and Sir Isaac Newton, in his day he was the most celebrated geographer and cartographer in the country, with many formidable achievements to his name including the mapping of India. In 1798, Rennell produced a map which, for the first time, revealed a mountain range in West Africa, called the Mountains of Kong. It appeared in his bestselling book, the text for which came from the vivid and detailed journals of the adventurer Mungo Park. The book was so influential that the newly discovered mountain range was incorporated into other maps from 1798 until 1892.[1]

In 1887, nearly six decades after Rennell's death, the French officer and explorer Louis Gustave-Binger set off on a mission to chart the course of the River Niger. To his astonishment, he discovered that the Mountains of Kong weren't where they were supposed to be, instead he found 'on the horizon, not even a ridge of hills! The Kong Mountain chain, which stretches across all the maps, never existed except in the imaginations of a few poorly informed explorers.'[2] As quickly as the mountain range had appeared on maps of the time, they now disappeared with everyone hoping that the embarrassment would quickly pass.

It just goes to show how easily we can come to accept something only to realize that there's not much there at all, if anything. It is, somewhat surprisingly, the feeling I had in exploring the topic of talent management, starting with trying to define it. Talent management is widely discussed, the topic of countless books and articles, taught in higher education establishments, practised by people in consultancies and in organizational departments. Yet, trying to find out what we are talking about is actually very difficult. There is much sharing that goes on about how to do it, what represents best practice in it, the tools to use in doing it. Despite all of that, there is a lacuna in terms of what 'it' is – it lacks definition. Just like the Mountains of Kong, talent management is reproduced by theorists and practitioners alike but it is somewhat surprising to find that despite the powerful arguments articulated in favour of it, without a definition we may not actually know what we're talking about.

A lot of energy is expended on the challenges of talent management, including the identification and development of future leaders. There are also actions about what effective talent management looks like. But these are general guidelines and principles rather than being anything specific to the idea of talent management.

Defining talent management

There have been attempts to define talent management but these are not consistent and they can be contradictory. The starting point for two researchers from India was to define the two words 'talent' and 'management' separately.[3]

According to the Oxford English Dictionary, talent is an old English word referring to a unit of weight or an amount of money. It's also a refers to 'a natural aptitude or skill' as well as referring to 'people possessing natural aptitude or skill'. Synonyms include 'flair, aptitude, facility, gift, knack, technique, touch, bent, ability, expertise, capacity, power, faculty; strength, strong point, forte, genius, brilliance; dexterity, adroitness, skill, cleverness, virtuosity, artistry'.

Management refers to 'the process of dealing with or controlling things or people'. Synonyms include 'administration, running, managing, organization, charge, care, direction, leadership, control, governing, governance, ruling, command, superintendence, supervision, overseeing, conduct, handling, guidance, operation'.

Putting these together we would reach the conclusion that talent management is the creation of a process for dealing with and controlling the people possessing natural aptitudes and skills. This barebones and minimalist definition is expanded elegantly by Bambhani and Saniy:

> Talent Management itself advocates managing the skill, competency, ability and power of employees within an organization. The concept is not constrained to hiring the right person at the right time, but it enlarges to exploring the unknown and remarkable qualities of your people and developing and nurturing them to obtain the desired outcome.[4]

Whilst recognizing that management is about administration and control, what they have done here is to recognize that it's also about the 'unknown and remarkable qualities of your people' and 'developing and nurturing'. Many of the practitioners of talent management seem to take it for granted that we will be focusing our time and resources on a select few individuals in our organizations; we will do that because we know about their performance and we have developed objective techniques that have identified their remarkable qualities.

What these practitioners and thought leaders in talent management have conspicuously missed is not only what Bambhani and Saniy referred to as the 'unknown' qualities, but also the people who remain unknown, unseen and under-recognized, having been ignored and sidelined because of our biases, which have impacted them long before they have encountered the objective processes of our technocratic psychology and assessment specialists.

Talent management is related to many other aspects of people processes and as a consequence there is a considerable overlap in the language that is used: as well as 'talent management', there is 'talent strategy', 'succession management', 'human resource planning'[5] and 'career planning'[6] are some of the terms that are used interchangeably.

According to eminent psychologists Stephen Woods and Michael West, talent management 'broadly refers to:

- Identification of key positions in the business that contribute to the achievement of strategic business objectives.
- Identification of high potential individuals, either externally or internally that can be developed and managed into those positions.'[7]

It's a frustrating exercise trying to find a universal and parsimonious definition of talent management. The quote is typical of what is written in that people describe what is done and the processes involved as opposed to what it actually is. Talent management entered the HR landscape as something completely different to what was normally done. However this is a sleight of hand: it's not a new way of viewing people in the organizations but instead it is a specific addition to the way that people are assessed, managed and developed.

There are essentially three themes to the descriptions of talent management:

1 It's a function within an organization. It may even be a sub-function of HR and people management generally. There are teams of people working within the talent management area and typically organizations will have a head of talent.

2 It is the associated processes which typically start with performance management, talent identification, talent assessment and talent development.

3 It is the people who the talent function, talent team and talent processes are targeted at. Here we find two principal yet fundamentally different approaches. The first focuses on identifying and developing those individuals who are the most talented – those who have the required qualities in greater abundance than others. Having identified these individuals, resources and time can then be expended on them. The other school of thought is that development should be provided more broadly so that everyone feels that they have opportunities to learn new skills and have new experiences.

The way people are treated and managed has developed and evolved over a long period of time so it is worth looking at how this occurred and the resonance earlier attitudes and beliefs have with the workplace today.

Prior to the Industrial Revolution, the way work was conducted changed very little. Work was carried out at home, and women were involved as much as men. However the formation of the guilds from the fifteenth century, started to see a separation of men and women, with the former being involved in more skilled work, typically requiring apprenticeships. Girls were able to be apprenticed but the number of trades that they were able to work in was fewer (19 compared to 143), of lower status and consequently lower paid. A distinction also started to be made between honourable and dishonourable work. Honourable work was conducted in towns, viewed as skilled and overseen by the guilds. Non-guild work was dishonourable as was working from home.[8] Today's attitudes about working from home have echoed down the years.

The Industrial Revolution was a great rupture from the past. Work became specialized, separated from activities at home and also led to the exclusion of middle-class women from the workplace. Professions, such as engineers, chemists and accountants, and their associated professional bodies were created. To have careers in these areas required education and as women were excluded from universities it meant that they were exclusively male.

Another, less prominent, profession quietly but rapidly also emerged at this time: management. The growth of large-scale businesses meant that there was an increasing need to organize the way in which work was carried out. Systems and processes were seen as being integral to this and the profession which had the most expertise and influence was engineering. Systemization and standardization brought many benefits – notably greater efficiency, reduced costs and more profit.

One of the drawbacks of this homogenization was that there was one way of doing things and anything else was seen as unacceptable. Henry Ford, frustrated by the pressure from salespeople to provide more customized cars for customers, decided to bring the discussions to an end:

> Therefore in 1909 I announced one morning, without any previous warning, that in the future we were going to build only one model, that the model was going to be 'Model T,' and that the chassis would be exactly the same for all cars, and I remarked: 'Any customer can have a car painted any colour that he wants so long as it is black.'

Not that this was a popular decision as he continued, 'I cannot say that anyone agreed with me.'[9]

There was a growing literature on management from the late 19th century onwards. In 1880 the New York Public library had no books on management. In 1881 the world's first management school opened in Philadelphia, and such was the interest in this new subject that by 1910 the library's shelves were groaning under the weight of 240 different books. The people most likely to find themselves in management positions were indeed engineers. In 1880 there were 3,000 engineers in America; by 1930 there were 300,000, of which two-thirds would end up in management positions.[10] The mindset of systems, processes and standardization meant there was little flexibility for individuals to express themselves. Scientific management also led to the development of personnel management which dealt with remuneration, record keeping, housing, health and welfare. The role of personnel management extended over the years to looking at training and selection of employees. From the 1930s onwards, psychological research emphasized the importance of looking at employee motivation and job satisfaction. Criticisms from management theorists, such as Peter Drucker, led to the renaming of personnel management to human resource management, and with it an acknowledgement that this was a function within an organization that needed to be accorded due recognition. Talent management came into the picture in the 1990s, and the term itself has been attributed to David Watkins of Softscape.[11]

Over this same period of time theories were formulated about how human beings could be classified into hierarchies. The 18th and 19th centuries saw the establishment of racial hierarchies which became an essential justification for the transatlantic slave trade. Disabled people, who had always been treated with suspicion and disdain, were subject to legislation in some parts of the world where they were banned from public spaces because they would make people feel uncomfortable. Referred to as the 'Ugly Laws', it meant separating disabled people from the rest of the population. A popular theory of the late 19th century was that of degeneracy. Those seen as degenerates included criminals, human rights activists, people with learning difficulties and homosexuals. The publication of the globally popular *Psychopathia Sexualis* in 1886 by William Krafft-Ebing laid the groundwork for the homophobic attitudes that we see in many regions of the world today. At the same time, laws were being introduced in many countries making homosexuality a criminal offence.

In other words, the birth of our modern-day organization set out to exclude women, disabled people, people of colour and LGBTQ+ individuals. Management was the purview of white, able-bodied, straight men – they were the special ones chosen to run our organizations.

Core principles of leadership and people management – or 'What have the Romans ever done for us?'

The reason it's so hard to find a specific set of principles that apply only to talent management is because it is part of the constant evolution of the way people are viewed and managed. The principles of human resource management will apply equally to the talent management function. For leaders and managers it would be worthwhile for them to consider the following 10 points:

1 Be available. Your people need to know that you are there to support and engage with them when needed.

2 Be civil to everyone and demonstrate emotional control. Be aware that your behaviour has an impact on your team, the way they respond to you and the way they work with one another. When you do this your team will always be more productive.

3 Listen to what your people are telling you. There is no need to become legalistic or contractual in the dealings with your team. Be

prepared to be flexible when necessary. Your team will appreciate you doing this.

4   Nevertheless you do need to have a framework and clear boundaries as to what is acceptable and unacceptable behaviour.

5   Be consistent in your dealings with people. And try to avoid chopping and changing things just for the sake of it. This is unsettling for your staff and will lead to a loss of productivity.

6   Make sure you select the right people who have the skills and abilities to do the work required and ideally have experience in the same field.

7   Provide feedback to those who are lazy and unproductive. Their slothfulness will be having an impact on the rest of the team.

8   Choose as leaders those who listen to the team members in order to find better ways of working and leading.

9   The leaders you choose are people that can be trusted and behave in an ethical fashion. They will understand what appropriate and inappropriate behaviour for someone in a senior role is.

I'm sure there's not much here that you would disagree with – they are useful principles that can guide a leader and manager's behaviour. What is possibly more surprising is that this is some of the advice given in a series of books written nearly 2,000 years ago by the Roman Lucius Iunius Moderatus Columella (d. *c.*70 AD).[12] His books provided comprehensive advice and guidance on agricultural management, including the treatment of slaves. His principal message was that if landowners treated their slaves well, then productivity would be higher. Today we would call this a win-win situation or enlightened self-interest.

The final and 10th point I wish to draw attention to is something that he considered to be very important for the person in charge:

10   'But, generally speaking, this above all else is to be required of him — that he shall not think that he knows what he does not know, and that he shall always be eager to learn what he is ignorant of.' A leader should have humility and the capability to learn new skills.

'Don't panic! Don't panic!': McKinsey and *The War for Talent*

The key publication, recognized by many, academics and practitioners alike, which provided the impetus for the explosion of interest in talent management is *The War for Talent*, published in 1998 and based on research carried out by the management consultancy McKinsey and Company.[13] I have always bracketed this research with a report published several years earlier from the Hudson Institute entitled *Workforce 2000*.[14] It is this report that I would like to focus on first.

Workforce 2000 looked at the changing demographics in the USA and how this would impact the economy, as well as organizational practice. The report identified a number of key trends: the economy would grow at a 'healthy pace' but manufacturing would shrink; the service sector would grow and require higher skill levels to succeed. The trend that captured the most attention was that 'The workforce will grow slowly, becoming older, more female, and more disadvantaged. Only 15% of the new entrants to the labour force over the next 13 years will be native white males compared to 47% in that category today.' (p. xiii)

The workforce was going to become more diverse than it had ever been, and it was as a result of this report that the concept of diversity took hold. Diversity functions were created to replace equal opportunity departments and diversity managers appeared on organizational role charts. Whilst there were key observations about the nature of work itself and America's place in the global economy, they had important insights into the increasing diversity of the workforce. Some of this today seems very much based on stereotypical assumptions, particularly when it came to older workers: 'as the average age of American workers climbs toward 40, the nation must ensure that its workforce and its institutions do not lose their adaptability and willingness to learn' (p. xiv).

There were important messages about organizations' mindsets towards women and minorities and the report recommended the need to:

- 'Reconcile the Conflicting Needs of Women, Work and Families: three fifths of all women over age 16 will be at work in the year

2000. Yet most current policies and institutions covering pay, fringe benefits, time away from work, pensions, welfare, and other issues were designed for a society in which men worked and women stayed home.

- Integrate Black and Hispanic Workers Fully into the Economy: the shrinking numbers of young people, at the rapid pace of industrial change, and the ever-rising skill requirements of the emerging economy make the task of fully utilising minority workers particularly urgent between now and 2000. Both cultural changes and education and training investments will be needed to create real equal employment opportunity.

- Improve the Educational Preparation of All Workers: as the economy grows more complex and more dependent on human capital, the standard set by the American education system must be raised.' (p. xiv)

McKinsey's *The War for Talent* was in part a reflection of the times with its emphasis on providing shareholder value at the expense of all other activities that an organization could engage in. For me, fairly or unfairly, it was also a panic-stricken response to *Workforce 2000*. The McKinsey report had no reference to diversity and inclusion within it, but instead was alarmed at the lack of talent available to organizations. However, research published at the time looking at what makes a successful executive concluded: 'The most objectively successful executive appears to be one who is a married, middle-aged white male whose spouse does not work outside the home, who has impressive educational credentials, and who displays a high commitment to his or her work.'[15] So perhaps we can see where the McKinsey anxiety was coming from.

McKinsey had carried out research in 77 large US companies and talked to HR departments examining how they carried out talent management, as well as conducting surveys of executives.

The language used to report their findings couldn't be more alarming:

'Companies are about to be engaged in a war for senior executive talent that will remain a defining characteristic of their competitive landscape for decades to come' 'a severe and worsening shortage of the people needed to run divisions and manage critical functions, let alone lead companies'

'at a time when the need for superior talent is increasing, big US companies are finding it difficult to attract and retain good people'

'All are vulnerable'

'Crisis'

'talent management is a burning priority'

It's as if Corporal Jones from the popular 1970s British sitcom *Dad's Army*, whose catchphrase was 'Don't panic! Don't panic!', was let loose on the final draft. The fact of the matter is that there was no shortage of talented people; whatever the proportion you think represents 'talent' had not changed. What had changed was the make-up of that pool of talented people which was now more diverse than it had ever been. In other words, the shortage that they were so concerned about was of white men who had, since the conception of management as a discipline within business, dominated the top jobs. It's an approach that has continued in the years since. There is very little reference to diversity, inclusion, minorities or discrimination in the talent management literature. It's as if it is of little concern to them. And yet it represents a significant problem for organizations as well as a great opportunity.

One of the biggest impacts that this report had was in terms of classifying the workforce into three categories: A, B and C. The A players, representing the top 20 per cent in the organization, are the star performers, the most 'talented' who need to be paid a lot more and developed quickly. The future of the organization depends on this group of people. And everything needs to be geared towards enabling this elite group to function in the way that they want. Rather than paying people for the role they are carrying out, they will be rewarded for who they are and the capabilities they are seen to possess. The B players, 70 per cent of people in the middle of the hierarchy, are individuals who you would keep and who need to be able to do the jobs allocated to them. The C players need to be moved on – they add little to the business and sap the energy and motivation of those around them. This 10 per cent of people need to be got rid of; as our McKinsey Corporal Jones states:

> The cost of carrying such people is enormous. Don't fool yourself that weeding them out will destroy morale; it's probably lower than you think already. Their low productivity drags down the performance of all they work with: teams go underdeveloped, and high performers get discouraged and leave. The weak performer ends up surrounded by a circle of weak performers, the ripple effects flow out across the organization, and the company's employee value proposition is damaged.

The poster boys for this approach were in the case studies that they enthusiastically provided, namely Enron and General Electric. The former was elegantly skewered by Malcolm Gladwell in a *New Yorker* article from 2002 entitled 'The Talent Myth'.[16] Former McKinsey consultant Jeff Skilling became CEO of Enron and then enacted the plan for talent that his former employers recommended. The free rein given to the most talented people led to a chaotic way of conducting business which ultimately led to its downfall, and to that of their auditors Arthur Andersen.

Jack Welch of GE was also a very public endorser of the War for Talent approach. He became a celebrity and something of a corporate superstar for the apparent rise and rise of a well-respected business in the United States. His reputation, however, is now being questioned and his legacy is undoubtedly tarnished. His commitment to paying A players significantly more than the rest benefited him enormously:

> And though Welch didn't start a company or invent a breakthrough new product, he earned millions of dollars, and tens of millions of dollars, then hundreds of millions of dollars, his net worth finally topping out at nearly \$1 billion landing him on Forbes's List of the 400 richest Americans. In retirement, GE picked up the tab for his apartment in the Trump International Hotel and tower, his meals at Michelin starred restaurants, his floor seats to Knicks games, and more.[17]

The other damaging impact that this approach has is that it sees talent as being a fixed characteristic of an individual. You either have it or you don't and adopting this view means that an organization's 'Focus is not to make everyone better, but to further develop those who are *already great*'[18] (emphasis added). In other words, greatness is there already, it exists and all we have to do is give those individuals the resources they need to become even greater. Failing to adopt this approach is sneeringly dismissed as 'politically correct'. This ignores completely research that shows adoption of a fixed mindset approach helps to limit people's view of their learning capabilities and ultimately has a detrimental impact on their performance. When people believe their capabilities can be developed, they will seek to stretch themselves and performance consequently improves.

This book will be looking not just at talent management techniques and processes – the technocratic approach to talent development – but also at the climate that exists within organizations that enables people to give their best, where they feel valued and included. Without this environment some people will never be considered as 'talent'. This isn't just about individuals showing their capabilities, but about being given the opportunities to be able to demonstrate them. I accept that there are a small number of people who have the talent, motivation and indeed luck to be able to enable their organizations to be successful now and in the future.

The argument in this book is that talent is not limited by gender, race, sexual orientation disability, class or any other dimension. And yet this is precisely what happens in organizations, which means that talent management programmes will always be less effective than they could be because they are not focused enough on tackling the problems and challenges inherent in identifying and developing talent from a diverse population of employees. They have been ill-served by talent management authors who have neglected almost completely diversity and inclusion.

Key points

One of the intentions with this Introduction was to provide a definition of talent management and in that I have singularly failed. The problem with talent management is that it's difficult to distinguish it clearly from typical HR practice. Instead, it is an evolution of HR practices and procedures over a period of time. Failure to recognize this will mean that HR splinters and is under-appreciated as a central function in organizations.[19]

The War for Talent report by McKinsey and Company was key in the growth of talent management. This highlighted their belief that organizations were not recruiting, developing and retaining their talent.

The recommendations they suggested led to a significant change in the way that people were managed in organizations: the most significant one being that the top 20 per cent should be remunerated not for the job they do but the 'talent' they possess. They should also be allowed greater freedom to enable them to make a contribution to the organization. These were known as the A players.

The B players were the 70 per cent of people who were doing a good job and should be encouraged to continue doing so and are worthwhile retaining. Meanwhile the remaining 10 per cent, designated as C players, had to be removed. This was as much for their own good as it was for the team they worked with, and the organization. By removing these people the organization would be doing them a favour, as it would enable them to find a job more suited to their capabilities.

The panic-stricken language of the report, as well as its title, was partly a response to a book written a few years earlier entitled *Workforce 2000* which outlined how the workforce of the new millennium was going to be much more diverse than it had been in the past. The pool of talent, identified as the top 20 per cent of people, however was never going to get any smaller but it was going to become more diverse. The McKinsey researchers and authors were not responding to a diminishing pool of talented people, which would never happen unless the population was declining, but it was instead an appeal to organizations about how they could ensure a consistent supply of white men to run them in the same way that they had done in the past.

The 18th and 19th centuries also saw ideas being developed that embedded racism into everyday thinking, excluded women and disabled people from our public spaces and vilified members of the LGBTQ+ community.

It is a surprise and a disappointment to find that many authors, academics and thought leaders in the area of talent management failed to address the issues of diversity and inclusion when it came to identifying leaders.

Notes

1 S Garfield and S Shepherd (2012) *On the Map: Why the world looks the way it does*, vol. 183, Profile Books, London

2 J Thomas. 'From the best authorities': The Mountains of Kong in the cartography of West Africa, *The Journal of African History*, 1991, 32 (3), 367–413

3 G Bhambhani and M Saniy. The emergence of talent management and diffusion of HRM, *EPRA International Journal of Research and Development (IJRD)*, 2017, 2 (7), 44–52

4 Ibid, p. 45

5 R E Lewis and R J Heckman. Talent management: A critical review, *Human Resource Management Review*, 2006, 16 (2), 139–54

6 E McKenna (2020) *Business Psychology and Organizational Behaviour*, Routledge

7 S A Woods and M A West (2020) *The Psychology of Work and Organizations*, 3rd edn, Cengage, p. 167

8 D Simonton (2013) *A History of European Women's Work*, Routledge

9 H Ford and S Crowther (1922) *My Life and Work*, Doubleday, p. 72

10 Y A Shenhav (2002) *Manufacturing Rationality*, Oxford University Press

11 G Bhambhani and M Saniy. The emergence of talent management and diffusion of HRM, *EPRA International Journal of Research and Development (IJRD)*, 2017, 2 (7), 44–52

12 Columella De Re Rustica, published in Vol. I of the Loeb Classical Library edition, 1941, https://penelope.uchicago.edu/Thayer/E/Roman/Texts/Columella/de_Re_Rustica/1*.html (archived at https://perma.cc/ZT5T-UHBG)

13 E G Chambers, M Foulon, H Handfield-Jones, S M Hankin and E G Michaels III. The war for talent, *The McKinsey Quarterly*, 1998 (3)

14 W B Johnston and A E Packer (1987) *Workforce 2000: Work and workers for the twenty-first century*, Hudson Institute

15   T A Judge, D M Cable, J W Boudreau and R D Bretz Jr. An empirical investigation of the predictors of executive career success, *Personnel Psychology*, 1995, 48 (3), 485–519

16   M Gladwell. The talent myth, *The New Yorker*, 2002, 22, 28–33

17   D Gelles (2022) *The Man Who Broke Capitalism: How Jack Welch gutted the heartland and crushed the soul of corporate America—and how to undo his legacy*, Simon and Schuster

18   T Chamorro-Premuzic (2017) *The talent delusion: Why data, not intuition, is the key to unlocking human potential*, Piatkus

19   C W Callaghan. Strategic human resources management or talent management: a theoretical non sequitur?, *Journal of Contemporary Management*, 2018, 15 (1), 763–83

2

The shackles of stereotypes

Here's a quick exercise I'd like you to undertake: imagine a carpenter. What colour is her hair? There is nothing about the word carpenter itself which either suggests a gender or hair colour. Nevertheless when asked a question like this it can take us by surprise because typically we will have imagined a man as carpenter and the hair as brown. This quick thought experiment was created out by the legal academic Gary Blasi[1] and demonstrates that for quite a lot of occupations and roles we have a picture in our heads of the type of person who will be carrying it out, something known as a prototype.

Writers on talent management consider one of their principal tasks is to describe the skills and qualities required of a leader. I am not decrying this, as it is clearly important and at Pearn Kandola we have our own leadership model. One of the things that these writers very rarely consider, however, is leadership prototypes because typically when people think of a leader it is a man that comes to mind. Let's also not forget that he's white. And straight.

Leadership prototypes impact who we consider to be a leader, and it will be the person who most closely matches that mental image. Of course, the fact that we hold that particular prototype is often based on our experience of leaders that we have encountered. The problem arises in how this prototype affects our judgement in determining who we think will be the leader of the future.

It's a two-stage process which involves first of all having an idea of what a leader does, the characteristics that they display and the impact they have. The second stage involves looking at a person and comparing their behaviour and appearance with our mind model of a leader. Bias can occur when the stereotypes we hold for some groups of people don't match our beliefs about the qualities needed to be a leader.[2]

The seminal study examining this phenomenon was carried out in the 1970s by Virginia Schein.[3] Three hundred middle managers were given a list of 92 adjectives and descriptive terms and asked to say which they thought applied to men in general, women in general and successful managers.

There was a high degree of overlap between the adjectives associated with men and the qualities needed for a successful manager. These included being:

- emotionally stable
- aggressive
- self-reliant
- vigorous
- objective
- well informed
- direct

As well as showing leadership ability and certainty the successful manager also needed to want responsibility and to take their role seriously.

The successful manager overlapped with the views of women in being:

- understanding
- helpful
- sophisticated
- aware of feelings of others
- intuitive
- neat

Furthermore women were not vulgar and held humanitarian values. Men were seen as the ones who took the lead and got things done, in other words they were agentic. Women, on the other hand, had strengths in the areas of relationships and empathy, in other words they were communal. This research gave us the expression 'think manager, think male', which sums up the leadership prototype model really well. The elegance and simplicity of the statement make it a useful slogan to apply to other characteristics too, as we will see.

This research was several decades ago and we would like to think, or even expect, that with more women in leadership roles the stereotypes and associations have changed. More recent meta-analyses have shown, however, that the associations between masculinity and leadership have not changed very much at all, with the observation that leaders are seen 'as quite similar to men but not very similar to women, as more agentic than communal, and as more masculine than feminine'.[4]

Gender stereotypes

One of the reasons why gender stereotypes are so stubborn and resistant to change is that we see men and women as having complementary roles as well as complementary qualities. Women have, since the Industrial Revolution, been seen as the homemakers and men as the breadwinners. This division of responsibilities has been justified by the belief that men and women have very different skills and personalities. It makes sense, using this argument, that men should be in the key positions in an organization as they have the necessary temperament and skills to fulfil the necessary role responsibilities. Gender stereotypes therefore are not just about how describing the various qualities of men and women (these are known as descriptive stereotypes) but also what they should or should not be, something known as prescriptive stereotypes. Prescriptive stereotypes are incredibly powerful in influencing people's choice of career. It's also important to bear in mind that these stereotypical beliefs are cultural phenomena, held by everyone in a particular society, and as a consequence it's not just men who hold such stereotypes but women too.

As women are seen to possess the traits of compassion, care and empathy (the descriptive stereotypes) it is right that they ought to be the ones who are the homemakers (the prescriptive stereotype). When women become mothers the expectation is that they will be the ones caring for their child. They will also be expected to be more understanding and compassionate with their colleagues at work. Doing these things and behaving in this way carries no particular reward apart from the general acceptance from others that they, women, are doing the right thing.

However, if they do not conform to the expectations of them, women will experience a backlash. When women behave in an agentic fashion, i.e. as men are expected to behave, they experience negative consequences (see Table 2.1).

It's a difficult line to tread. If you want to be liked by your colleagues and your boss, then you should behave in ways that are more stereotypically female.

Unfortunately, the price that will be paid for being liked is the perception that you do not possess the requisite qualities to be a leader. Adopt assertive, confident, strategic behaviours and you won't be seen as 'female' enough and so negative views will be formed of you. The research shows that where women don't conform to the prescriptions they are more likely to have negative qualities attributed to them such as being cold, selfish, devious and hostile.

I was working with a bank who asked me to run a session on gender bias with a new intake of graduates. As part of the session I presented them with a case study of someone in charge of the team who was displaying the qualities required of a leader: assertive, confident but also aggressive and very direct with feedback. There were over 100 people in the session and I asked them how competent they thought the person was and how much they liked them.

TABLE 2.1 Summary of the consequences of violating prescriptive stereotypes[5]

Consequences	Impact
• Reduced social acceptance	• Less likely to be hired
• Reduced liking	• Reduced influence
• Seen as cold, selfish, devious, hostile	• Increased sexism
• Not a good team member	

Most people in the room said the individual was competent but the room was evenly divided on whether the person was likable. The reason for this was that whilst all of the details were the same, half of the group had a leader called John and for the other half the leader was called Joan. The male leader was seen as marginally more competent than the female. However, Joan was intensely disliked for her assertive behaviour, which was seen as intimidating, whereas John was commended for it; indeed people thought that they could learn from somebody as demanding as him.

The gender of the individual completely changed the perception of them as a leader, something referred to as double standards. This is something that is critically important to remember when 360-degree feedback is carried out, for example. I clearly remember having a meeting with a client who I had known for quite a number of years. She was senior in HR and ambitious to go further but on this occasion she wasn't her normal cheerful, positive self. On enquiring if she was alright, she eventually told me that she had just the day before returned from a three-day leadership programme run by her company.

She was the only woman on the programme and part of the timetable was given over to people giving feedback to one another. From behind a cupboard, where she had deposited the sheets of flipchart paper which contained her feedback, she showed me what had been written about her. What I read was barely credible and the comments bore no resemblance to the individual that I had known and worked with for several years. 'Needs to listen to what people are saying', 'too directive', 'lacks basic understanding of finance' and perhaps most damning of all 'the lights are on but there's no one at home'. I wasn't the only one who couldn't understand the feedback, she was clearly confused and upset.

She asked me what she should do with the outputs from the leadership session and I told her to throw them away – there's no point even keeping them behind the cupboard. There was no doubt that the feedback she had been given was sexist, designed to undermine her leadership credentials and, if she had listened to it, could have stalled her career indefinitely. Instead, what she decided to do was to leave the organization and took on an executive committee position at another business.

At the time of writing the 2024 US presidential election is taking place and it's fascinating to see how the descriptive and prescriptive stereotypes can be seen already in the opinion polls asking people to rate the qualities of Vice President Kamala Harris and former president Donald Trump.

Vice President Harris's positive traits, where she scored higher than the former president, were: compassionate, honest and intelligent. Trump outscored his opponent on being charismatic, a strong leader, authentic, a better communicator, likable, qualified and competent.[6] Strength and competence as a leader come through for Trump, with Harris scoring more highly in the people-related area. The descriptive stereotypes of women and of leaders can clearly be seen here.

During the campaign the prescriptions expected of women were also on display. Trump's running mate, Senator JD Vance, had shared his very clear views about the role of women in an interview with Fox News host Tucker Carlson in 2021, where he said the country was being run by Democrats, corporate oligarchs and 'a bunch of childless cat ladies who are miserable at their own lives and the choices that they've made and so they want to make the rest of the country miserable, too'.

'It's just a basic fact – you look at Kamala Harris, Pete Buttigieg, AOC [Alexandria Ocasio-Cortez] – the entire future of the Democrats is controlled by people without children,' Vance continued. 'And how does it make any sense that we've turned our country over to people who don't really have a direct stake in it?'[7]

The three people he mentioned included two women of colour and a gay man. This is another manifestation of a prescriptive stereotype outlining what a woman's role is and a criticism that has been levelled at several female politicians in recent times. In 2016 in the UK the Prime Minister David Cameron had just resigned. Andrea Leadsom, who was standing to become the Conservative Party's new leader in the UK, and consequently the new prime minister, said that as a mother of three she had 'a very real stake' in the future of the country. Her comment which was similar in tone and intent to Vance's was seen as a pointed reference to her opponent, Theresa May, who had no children. The criticism Leadsom received eventually led to her dropping out of the race. In Australia, Julia Gillard, the former prime minister, was described as being 'deliberately barren' as well as 'a childless, atheist ex-communist' with the latter comments coming from a member of her own party.[8] It's part of a long-standing misogynistic view that women should not be participating in the public realm. Their role is to be in the background, being supportive, bearing children and, above all, being quiet.

This is also indicative of what is known as the double bind that women face. This is when a woman behaves in line with the prescriptive stereotypes and has children and the expectation is that she will be the principal carer. This then means less time to engage in the leadership role. Choosing to have a career will bring out greater hostility.[9]

The double bind also extends to the behaviours that women in leadership roles can and cannot display in the workplace, which creates dilemmas[10] such as:

- Being seen as either too soft or too tough. Acting in a way that is too soft will conform to the stereotype of a woman as being more caring and sensitive. This will mean that she will be liked more. Acting tough will be seen as more leader-like which again doesn't fit the stereotype of a woman and so a backlash will be experienced.

- Having to be better than male peers to be considered as having the potential to progress to leadership. There is, in effect, a higher standard that women have to reach in order to be viewed as a leader of the future.

Progress has undoubtedly been made in terms of discrimination against women but significant barriers still exist. Measuring performance, identifying leadership potential and determining effectiveness as a leader remain problematic for the assessment of women at work.

Disability

Far less research has been carried out in the area of disability at work compared to gender and race. From what we do know, however, disabled people experience barriers and obstacles in terms of progressing to leadership positions.

It has been estimated by the World Health Organization (WHO) that there are approximately 1 billion people who are disabled. Many will have an injury of sorts for a short period of time and will experience temporary impairments. Some of these will become lasting impairments but it is the interaction with the world around us that creates the disability. For example, a wheelchair user becomes disabled when they are faced with steps to enter a building rather than a ramp. The United Nations Convention on the Rights of Persons with Disabilities adopts this approach recognizing the significance of the interaction between a person having an impairment and the environment they are in. The barriers that exist for disabled people include ones that are physical, but of more interest here are the attitudinal ones that get in the way of disabled people progressing within organizations. There is also a hierarchy, with those who have mental or learning disabilities being perceived less positively than those with physical ones.[11]

Disabled people experience slower promotion rates than people without a disability, with one of the earliest studies of this kind carried out in 1980.[12] Later studies including one by the Equal Employment Opportunities Commission in the United States,[13] the background to which was the declining number, as well as percentage, of disabled people working in federal government. One of the barriers identified was that 'unfounded fears, myths and stereotypes persist regarding the employment of people with disabilities. These beliefs may unlawfully influence some employment decisions.' (p. vi) The report found that disabled people were overrepresented in the lower grades (51 per cent compared to 32 per cent for the workforce as a whole) and were earning less. They were also leaving the federal workforce at a faster rate than they were being recruited and one important reason behind this was the lack of opportunity to progress and be promoted. Between 2002 and 2006 the number of disabled people who were promoted actually went down by over 25 per cent. In that same period 3 per cent more people without disabilities were promoted. One of the reasons for this was that 'myths and stereotypes about people with disabilities persist... Some officials believe that people with disabilities are not as well qualified as those without disabilities' (p, 25) and as a result they are not getting jobs at a suitable level.

Other researchers found that disabled people have lower job satisfaction which was related to more negative views about their treatment by their line manager and job insecurity.[14]

In 2012 the European community recognized that inclusion was important for economic growth and stated: 'inclusive growth also means paying particular attention to the needs of people with disabilities so that they can benefit from the single market'[15] (p. 6). It's important therefore that disabled people are able to find employment in line with their abilities, experience and qualifications.

Anxiety and disability

There are two overriding factors which also need to be considered for disabled people who have disabilities that are visible to others. They are referred to as anxieties and the first is existential anxiety. The theory is that meeting people with a visible disability reminds us of how vulnerable we are and how precarious existence is. One misjudgement or an accident could result in any of us having a disability. It's as fragile as having our skin punctured by the wrong sort of needle or an insect. We try to push away the thoughts that led to these uncomfortable feelings, but in addition to that we also try to remove ourselves from the person who led us to think this way. Second is aesthetic anxiety which relates to how people look. We have a notion of what is considered beautiful and even normal. Essentially, we prefer people who are more or less symmetrical and who are not disfigured, especially in the areas where we pay most attention such as the face and neck.

Both of these forms of anxiety lead us to not want to have contact with disabled people. It's very important that these feelings of discomfort are discussed in the workplace because they are at the heart of the prejudices that we hold toward disabled people.

Internal or external attribution of disability

Then there are the labels which get in the way of being able to see the individual and their actual performance. Definitions of disability in legislation and policies recognize that it's an interaction between a person's impairment and their environment. If a person is given the reasonable adjustments to perform the job to the standard required, then the impairment will not create any obstacles in carrying out their work. The adjustments might be, for example, providing a larger computer screen, or allowing someone to work from home on a regular basis. Therefore in this case, disability is viewed as something that is external to the individual.

If disability is seen as an illness, then it is internal to the person, part of who they are, which then affects assessments of other aspects of their character and competence. You can see this in stories, movies and the media generally where there are pronounced tendencies to view people with disabilities as evil and villainous; Shakespeare's Richard III being one notable example.

Stereotypes about disabled people

Stereotypes about any group of people vary on two dimensions: warmth (i.e. extent to which we find people from that group likeable, friendly and honest) and competence (i.e. qualified, skilled, intelligent, ambitious).[16] Disabled people are seen as likable but low on competence; in other words, people will feel positively towards them but also see them as not particularly talented or skilled.

This is revealed in the positive and negative stereotypes which are held about disabled people. The positives include being 'courageous, heroic, hard-working, persistent, conscientious, honest, moral, and friendly'. However, the negatives are being seen as 'dependent, incompetent, unemployable, passive, and weak'.[17] When these two aspects are combined, it means that the emotional reactions towards people with disabilities are of pity and paternalism.

People who, generally speaking, hold positive attitudes towards disabled people will, when under pressure, continue to be friendly towards them, but be harsher and more critical in judging their competence. This shows that even when we hold positive attitudes these can change should we be faced with greater stress.[18] Studies examining implicit attitudes towards people with disabilities found the same result – that they were viewed as being low on competence and high on warmth. Competence, however, is also context-specific for disabled people because they are viewed as being more competent outside of the workplace than in it.[19] The authors of the study suggest this may explain why disabled people garner more support for equal rights campaigning outside of the workplace, but in a working environment are more likely to be sidelined

Studies have shown that neurodivergent individuals are seen as less intelligent, less attractive, less enthusiastic and are less likely to be successful in the future.[20] Surprisingly, even those professionals working with neurodivergent individuals had the same attitudes as the general public. Furthermore neurodivergent individuals were not seen as 'normal' and generally speaking it was seen as some form of illness. Approximately 40 per cent of people thought that neurodivergent individuals would have difficulty in forming personal relationships.

It is interesting to see that whilst disabled people are typically viewed as not having the qualities to become leaders, they are more likely to have their own businesses, to display entrepreneurial qualities as well as developing the skills required to run and lead a business successfully.[21] Being entrepreneurs they have the opportunity and the freedom to work in the way that they want, which those working in an organization don't necessarily have. Part of the reason why more disabled people are self-employed is because they feel they have no choice in order to avoid the discrimination they face. However, 'personal ambition and desire'[22] are also important motivational drivers that provide an alternative picture of the competence of disabled people than is typically gained in organizations. This raises the question as to why disabled people are viewed more favourably when they are outside of an organization than when they are in it. It also shows that being self-employed enables disabled people to display more of their leadership qualities than they would be able to if they were employed.

Race

More research has been carried out on race and racism than on disability and as a consequence we know more about the stereotypes that are held and the impact it has on decisions that are made in the workplace.

Ingenious methods of measuring racial attitudes have had to be devised because this has become a very sensitive topic to be discussed in the workplace. Often there is a difference in the results from traditional surveys of attitudes and from measures of implicit bias. It's a measure of the progress that's been made that many of us don't think it's acceptable to hold racist attitudes or express them publicly. Such surveys have shown a notable reduction in racist attitudes towards minorities in many countries. Whilst this is to be welcomed it's probably not as great as it would appear. In one ingenious study, participants had to complete a survey measuring their racial attitudes. One group was hooked up, via an elaborate system of wires, to a machine which the researchers said could tell whether they were answering the survey honestly. The other group of people filled out the survey in the usual way. The equipment, as well as the explanation, were bogus, as the machinery provided no read-out on people's attitudes at all. Nevertheless, it did have an impact on the people completing the surveys because those hooked up to the truth-telling machine gave responses in line with the stereotypes of racial groups. The participants in the other group actually gave answers which showed that they held less racist views. The study was carried out in 1971, which just goes to show that even then race was becoming a sensitive topic, where impression management on these topics was becoming more important. I really like the title of the paper, incidentally: 'Current stereotypes: A little fading, a little faking'.[23]

Asians (and much of the work on this has been done on Asian Americans) have achieved high levels of education attainment compared to other groups. However, this has not translated into an advantage in the workplace, particularly in moving into leadership positions.

Advantages that are gained by cultural background in terms of education do not play so big a part once someone is in the workplace. So despite the apparent success of the group, in the workplace, Asians are underachieving.[24] This is referred to as a 'bamboo ceiling' (obviously adapted from the glass ceiling used to describe the lack of progress made by women into senior roles).

Sociologist Tiffany Huang summarized some of the obstacles faced by Asian people trying to enter the workplace, which included lack of informal networks compared to their white peers, lack of family connections within certain sectors, stereotyping and discrimination. On the stereotype contact model, Asians are seen as competent but lacking in warmth. The emotions associated with this combination are envy and resentment.

Furthermore, in my experience I have found that there is far less concern about discrimination faced by Asians in the workplace than for other groups. The same applies to Jewish people who also have this combination of competence and lack of warmth. During the pandemic I conducted research into the rise of anti-Chinese prejudice, or Sinophobia, in the United Kingdom. This was prior to lockdown, which happened in March of that year, and up until then the respondents to our survey said that they had experienced a 50 per cent increase in prejudice against them. Many of the people who had experienced this racism remarked how little support they received from colleagues in the workplace, leaving them feeling isolated and alone. It's also worth mentioning that the racism they experienced wasn't just from white people but also from other minority groups including African Caribbean individuals and people from the Indian subcontinent.

The competent but not warm stereotype combination means that Asians are considered suitable for some roles but not others. Usually, they will be found in technical positions and not in general management roles. Asians are seen as having a good education, possessing specific technical skills and being highly numerate. Stereotypically, they are also seen as having poor people skills due to their more subservient and passive nature. Having to deal with these stereotypes and attempt to ensure that people don't view them in this way puts an additional burden on these employees' shoulders that white staff don't experience.

There are very long-standing stereotypes associated with black people. On the competence and warmth matrix, poor black people lack both competence and warmth, much like all poor people. Middle-class black people, however, are on the midpoint for both dimensions. Commonly held stereotypes today have in fact been prevalent for many centuries since the advent of the transatlantic slave trade. In 1788 *The Gentleman's Magazine* published an article which described 'the Negro':

> possessed of passions not only strong but ungovernable; a mind
> dauntless, warlike and unmerciful; a temper extremely irascible; a
> disposition indolent, selfish and deceitful; fond of joyous sociality,
> riotous mirth and extravagant shew... Furious in his love as in his hate;
> at best, a terrible husband, a harsh father and a precarious friend.[25]

Physically strong, unreliable, untrustworthy, fun loving, a poor father and husband, ruled by emotions. This stereotype that we can recognize today was already formed over 200 years ago; attitudes are clearly changing but not as quickly as we might like to think. There are very few black people in senior positions in organizations today. The leadership prototype research has a distinct pro white bias. When people are told that an organization is diverse but not told how this distributed, they will typically identify the leaders as white and those in the lower ranks from minority groups.[26] Using more fiendishly clever techniques, recent research has found that we still associate leaders with white people.[27]

As we know in the talent management field it's not just about how we see leaders now but also about identifying the people who will be leaders in the future, the people who have the potential to ascend to leadership roles. How individuals manage a team, inspire them and essentially behave in leader-like ways now is how people are judged on their suitability to enter high potential programmes. To display leadership qualities, however, is partly the result of individuals making it clear that they are in charge, in effect saying to themselves and others 'I am the leader'. That's only one part of the equation – the other part is for the team members, those who report into the leader, to accept that person, by in effect saying, 'You are the leader'.

As there is a pro-white bias for people in leadership, anyone from a minority group will feel like less of a match to the leadership prototype, which in turn leads to some unfortunate consequences. Lack of acceptance of a minority as leader will be shown in the things people say as well as how they behave.

When white team members have a leader who is also white their own body language is more constrained, accepting and recognizing their role as followers. It's not about subservience but more a reflection of their respect. With minority leaders they are far less likely to be shown the respect accorded to white peers, which will lead to them having their competence questioned.[28] Minority leaders will also be undermined by team members talking amongst themselves about the inadequacy of the person in charge of them. They can also do this, it has been observed, by going behind the leader's back to get advice on how to tackle a piece of work from other senior people who they know in the organization, maybe even including the previous leader.[29] All of this erodes the minority leader's effectiveness, confidence and credibility within the organization.

This is something that I have observed in discussions with people in coaching conversations: this constant sense that minority leaders have to continue proving themselves to their own team members. This lack of acceptance will be seen by their own boss who will conclude, based on what they have seen, that this person is not able to manage a team.

At the end of a conference where I had share research on the difficulties minorities face as leaders, I was approached by a very senior leader working in the public sector in the UK. She recognized exactly what I was talking about and it helped her to understand what was going on within her team and the difficulties that she was experiencing. On one occasion she had written a letter to a high-ranking government minister which she had handed over to her PA to type and then to send. A few days later she was talking with her PA and expressing surprise that she had not received a reply from the minister, only to find that the letter had never been sent. Asking for the reason for this she was told that the PA did not think the letter was written to the standard required of the department. This was a highly educated individual who had, before joining the civil service, had a very successful career as a barrister. Her response to this startling piece of news was to question her literacy and reasoning skills.

This one piece of obstructive behaviour had led her to question her abilities, and had made her look inefficient in the eyes of a significant, senior stakeholder. It is by such actions that careers can be stalled and is more likely to happen to people who don't fit the leadership prototype.

LGBTQ+

The acronym LGBTQ+ contains a number of separate identities, each of which has its own stereotypes associated with it. A short account like this won't do it justice but hopefully I can give you a flavour of some of the challenges and obstacles that members of this community face.

It's important to recognize that in a significant number of countries around the world it is illegal to have same sex relationships. In a smaller number of countries, where someone is in such a relationship, the penalty is death. It's important for multinational organizations to appreciate just how difficult it must be for some of their colleagues working in such locations if they have an LGBTQ+ identity.

For the best part of 100 years, from the late 19th century through much of the 20th century, attitudes towards LGBTQ+ individuals has been very damning. In addition to the legislation, being attracted to someone of the same sex came to be seen as an illness. Theories developed in the late 19th century saw it as a form of degeneracy and it was likened to a disease which could, if left to its own devices, lead to the downfall of civilization as we knew it. The American Psychiatric Association in 1953 published the first edition of the DSM, Diagnostic and Statistical Manual, which described the indicators that professionals should be looking out for in order to diagnose psychiatric disorders. One of those disorders was homosexuality. It was eventually removed from the DSM in the early 21st century. The WHO

(World Health Organization) removed it as an illness in the early 1990s. Damaging, homophobic and prejudiced attitudes towards members of the LGBTQ+ community have been endorsed by religious leaders, medical professionals, legislators and societies. It should be no surprise then to find that, for all the colour and celebrations around Pride events, there are still very negative views held about LGBTQ+ individuals including that they are mentally ill[30] and abnormal.[31]

Gay men were the focus of much research at first with attitude scales such as the Attitudes Toward Lesbians and Gay Men Scale[32] and the Homosexuality Attitudes Scale[33] being developed. These revealed the strength and depth of homophobic attitudes throughout society. As an invisible identity, it meant that many people would remain in the closet, and in many cases attempted to deny to themselves their true sexual orientation.

Later measures were also developed including the Modern Homonegativity Scale.[34] These measures are more traditional with respondents having to answer questions in a survey. These give an indication of explicit attitudes, but what they provide doesn't necessarily give a full measure of attitudes because of impression management. Implicit, or unconscious, attitudes are assessed by a variety of other techniques, the most popular and well researched of which is the Implicit Association Test (IAT). In many countries there has undoubtedly been a change in attitudes with greater tolerance being displayed towards those belonging to a minority sexual orientation. Surveys of the IAT data, however, reveal quite strong implicit biases towards people who are heterosexual. An examination of the data from 2002 to 2006 showed 68 per cent of people having a pro-heterosexual bias.[35] A further examination looking at data from 2006 to 2012 found that this heterosexual preference had persisted.[36]

When we look specifically at the stereotypes, what emerges very strongly, particularly for lesbians and gay men, is that for each group the stereotypes are the reverse of what we find for heterosexual men and women. So the characteristics associated with heterosexual men are more likely to be applied to lesbians. The characteristics associated with women are more closely associated with gay men. In other words the stereotypical view of lesbians is that they are more masculine, and the stereotypical view of gay men is that they are more feminine.[37] In terms of the Stereotype Content Model lesbians are seen as more competent than gay men, but gay men are seen as being warmer than lesbians.[38] These stereotypical views of gay men and lesbians are in fact also held by gay men and lesbians.[39] The reversal of the stereotypes was first highlighted in 1987 with the development of what is called the Implicit Inversion Theory.[40] It's fascinating to realize that one's views of a male and female, who we might assume to be heterosexual, will be completely reversed on learning that they are gay or lesbian.[41]

Media representations of gay men and lesbians reinforce these stereotypes to such an extent that we readily accept them. Heteronormativity is something that refers to the assumptions that we make that everybody is heterosexual unless we learn otherwise. The stereotypes of gay men and lesbians in particular are so strong that it has led to the creation of the concept of homonormativity,[42] where we expect gay men and lesbians to conform to that way of behaving.

More research into how LGBTQ+ individuals are perceived has shown that the stereotypes for lesbians and gay men in particular are becoming more androgynous, in other words they possess a mix of stereotypical masculine and feminine characteristics.[43]

People from the LGBTQ+ community recognize that there is diversity within each of these identities.[44] However, rather than challenging the overall stereotype subtypes have been created, such as hyper-masculine gay men[45] and lipstick lesbians.[46] The effect of this however is that the predominant stereotype associating gay men with femininity and lesbians with masculinity remains intact.

One consequence of the inversion of the stereotypes is that in terms of leadership roles gay men are viewed in much the same way the women are, and lesbians in a similar way to heterosexual men. Consequently, when compared to the leadership prototype it is lesbian women who fit it more closely than gay men.[47] The neat epithet 'think manager – think male' has, unsurprisingly, been refashioned to 'think manager – think heterosexual male'.[48]

Within LGBTQ+ most research has been carried out on lesbians and gay men, with the other identities having been omitted from any serious investigation. This is changing slowly and we are getting an idea about the stereotypes associated with the other identities such as bisexuality and transgender.

What we do know is that these other identities are treated with a lot more suspicion; for example, bisexuals are seen as 'disingenuous', 'dishonest', 'indecisive', 'confused' and 'selfish'. The overall message is that if these individuals cannot accept that they are gay, how can we ever trust them with anything else that they say?[49] These attitudes towards people who are bisexual are held by lesbians and gay men as well as heterosexuals.[50]

Stereotypes of transgender and non-binary individuals reveal that they are seen as outcasts and aliens,[51] mentally ill, abnormal, having difficulty with self-acceptance.[52,53]

Reinforcing the idea of the gender hierarchy with men at the top and women at the bottom, it has also been found to be the case with transgender individuals. Those who have transitioned from female to male found that they were afforded greater respect and status,[54] whereas those who transitioned from male to female felt that they were less valued.[55]

Key points

Talent management does not exist within a vacuum. The stereotypes that exist about different groups in society impact the way people are treated in organizations and the decisions that are made about them. To believe anything else is to bury your head in the sand.

The qualities of leaders most readily match the stereotypes of white men. The stereotypes of other groups that I have described in this chapter, including women, disabled people, ethnic minorities and LGBTQ+ individuals, show that none of them match the leadership prototype.

There are difficulties that the groups I have described in this chapter face in the workplace in terms of how they express themselves. In some instances they have to tread a fine line between acting like a leader and conforming to the stereotypes of the group. In other cases they're just seen as not being up to the job of being a leader.

It isn't just those whose job it is to identify future leaders who are affected but also the team members who are being managed by these individuals. The way they behave towards their manager will be also depend on how closely they fit the leadership prototype. Where the leader doesn't fit the stereotype of a leader, they will experience greater difficulties.

Notes

1 G Blasi. Advocacy against the stereotype: Lessons from cognitive social psychology, *UCLA Law Review*, 2002, 49(5), 1241–82

2 A H Eagly and S J Karau. Role congruity theory of prejudice toward female leaders, *Psychological Review*, 2002, 109 (3), 573–98

3 V E Schein. The relationship between sex role stereotypes and requisite management characteristics, *Journal of Applied Psychology*, 1973 (April), 57 (2), 95

4 A M Koenig, A H Eagly, A A Mitchell and T Ristikari. Are leader stereotypes masculine? A meta-analysis of three research paradigms, *Psychological Bulletin*, 2011, 137 (4), 616–42, p. 634

5 B Kandola and J Kandola (2013) *The Invention of Difference: The story of gender bias at work*, Pearn Kandola Publishing

6 T Orth. Harris vs. Trump: How Americans evaluate them on personality and policy, YouGov.com, 22 July 2024, https://today.yougov.com/politics/ articles/50144-harris-vs-trump-americans-evaluate-personality-and-policy (archived at https://perma.cc/H5U3-KS44)

7 R Treisman. JD Vance went viral for 'cat lady' comments. The centuries-old trope has a long tail, NPR, 29 July 2024, www.npr.org/2024/07/29/nx-s1-5055616/jd-vance-childless-cat-lady-history (archived at https://perma. cc/6DKR-29J8)

8 N Eggert. Female politicians and babies: a lose-lose situation? BBC News, 2 August 2017, www.bbc.co.uk/news/world-40800687 (archived at https:// perma.cc/8UD9-S2DE).

9 D L Teele, J Kalla and F Rosenbluth. The ties that double bind: social roles and women's underrepresentation in politics, *American Political Science Review*, 2018, 112 (3), 525–41

10 Catalyst (Organization) (2007) *The Double-Bind Dilemma for Women in Leadership: Damned if you do, doomed if you don't*, Catalyst

11 P Harpur, U Connolly and P Blanck. Socially constructed hierarchies of impairments: the case of Australian and Irish workers' access to compensation for injuries, *Journal of Occupational Rehabilitation*, 2017, 27, 507–19

12 R B Bressler and A W Lacy. An analysis of the relative job progression of the perceptibly physically handicapped, *Academy of Management Journal*, 1980, 23 (1), 132–43

13 US Equal Employment Opportunity Commission. Improving the participation rate of people with targeted disabilities in the federal work force, 15 January 2008, http://whitehouse.gov/news/freedominitiative.html (archived at https://perma.cc/U8ZC-NZZY).

14 L Schur, K Han, A Kim, M Ameri, P Blanck and D Kruse. Disability at work: A look back and forward, *Journal of Occupational Rehabilitation*, 2017, 27, 482–97

15 S M Act 2011. Communication from the Commission to the European Parliament, the Council, the Economic and Social Committee and the Committee of the Regions

16 S T Fiske, A J C Cuddy, P Glick and J Xu. A model of (often mixed) stereotype content: Competence and warmth respectively follow from perceived status and competition, *Journal of Personality and Social Psychology*, 2002, 82, 878–902, doi:10.1037/0022-3514.82.6.878 (archived at https://perma.cc/45PN-A9AV)

17 O Rohmer and E Louvet. Implicit stereotyping against people with disability, *Group Processes & Intergroup Relations*, 2018, 21 (1), 127–40, p. 128

18 P T Nelissen, U R Hülsheger, G M van Ruitenbeek and F R Zijlstra. How and when stereotypes relate to inclusive behavior toward people with disabilities, *The International Journal of Human Resource Management*, 2016, 27 (14), 1610–25

19 O Rohmer and E Louvet. Implicit stereotyping against people with disability, *Group Processes & Intergroup Relations*, 2018, 21 (1), 127–40

20 G Jamal. Stereotypes about adults with learning disabilities: are professionals a cut above the rest?, *Disability, CBR & Inclusive Development*, 2019, 30 (2), 7–36

21 M K Jones and P L Latreille. Disability and self-employment: evidence for the UK, *Applied Economics*, 2011, 43 (27), 4161–78

22 A Maritz and R Laferriere. Entrepreneurship and self-employment for people with disabilities, *Australian Journal of Career Development*, 2016, 25 (2), 45–54, p. 52

23 H Sigall and R Page. Current stereotypes: A little fading, a little faking, *Journal of Personality and Social Psychology*, 1971, 18 (2), 247

24 T J Huang. Negotiating the workplace: second-generation Asian American professionals' early experiences, *Journal of Ethnic and Migration Studies*,

2020, 47 (11), 2477–96, https://doi.org/10.1080/1369183X.2020.1778455 (archived at https://perma.cc/2TKD-U396)

25 P Jackson (1989) *Maps of Meaning: An introduction to cultural geography*, Routledge, p. 135

26 A S Rosette, G H Leonardelli and K W Phillips. The White standard: racial bias in leader categorization, *Journal of Applied Psychology*, 2008, 93 (4), 758

27 C D Petsko and A S Rosette. Are leaders still presumed white by default? Racial bias in leader categorization revisited, *Journal of Applied Psychology*, 2023, 108 (2), 330

28 D S DeRue and S J Ashford. Who will lead and who will follow? A social process of leadership identity construction in organizations, *Academy of Management Review*, 2010, 35 (4), 627–47

29 S Nkomo. Moving from the letter of the law to the spirit of the law: the challenges of realising the intent of employment equity and affirmative action, *Transformation: Critical Perspectives on Southern Africa*, 2011, 77 (1), 122–35

30 E E Levitt and A D Klassen. Public attitudes toward homosexuality: Part of the 1970 national survey by the Institute for Sex Research, *Journal of Homosexuality*, 1974, 1, 29–43

31 S Madon. What do people believe about gay males? A study of stereotype content and strength, *Sex Roles*, 1997, 37, 663–85

32 G M Herek. Heterosexuals' attitudes toward lesbians and gay men: correlates and gender differences, *Journal of Sex Research*, 1988, 25, 451–77

33 M Kite. Psychometric properties of the Homosexuality Attitude Scale, *Representative Research in Social Psychology*, 1992, 19, 79–94

34 M A Morrison and T G Morrison. Development and validation of a scale measuring modern prejudice toward gay men and lesbian women, *Journal of Homosexuality*, 2002, 43 (2), 15–37

35 B A Nosek, F L Smyth, J J Hansen, T Devos, N M Lindner, K A Ranganath and M R Banaji. Pervasiveness and correlates of implicit attitudes and stereotypes, *European Review of Social Psychology*, 2007, 18, 36–88

36 J A Sabin, R G Riskind and B A Nosek. Health care providers' implicit and explicit attitudes toward lesbian women and gay men, *American Journal of Public Health*, 2015, 105 (9), 1831–41, https://doi.org/10.2105/AJPH.2015.302631 (archived at https://perma.cc/HZ7B-5SZE)

37 A J Blashill and K K Powlishta. Gay stereotypes: the use of sexual orientation as a cue for gender-related attributes, *Sex Roles*, 2009, 61, 783–93

38 A A Vaughn, S A Teeters, M S Sadler and S B Cronan. Stereotypes, emotions, and behaviors toward lesbians, gay men, bisexual women, and bisexual men, *Journal of Homosexuality*, 2017, 64 (13), 1890–911, https://doi.org/10.1080/00918369.2016.1273718 (archived at https://perma.cc/2TKD-U396)

39 H M Clarke and K A Arnold. Diversity in gender stereotypes? A comparison of heterosexual, gay and lesbian perspectives, *Canadian Journal of*

Administrative Sciences, 2017, 34, 149–58, https://doi.org/10.1002/cjas.1437 (archived at https://perma.cc/HXF8-XH4D)

40 M E Kite and K Deaux. Gender belief systems: homosexuality and the implicit inversion theory, *Psychology of Women Quarterly*, 1987, 11, 83–96

41 R J Barrantes and A A Eaton. Sexual orientation and leadership suitability: how being a gay man affects perceptions of fit in gender-stereotyped positions, *Sex Roles*, 2018, 1–16

42 L Duggan (2002) The new homonormativity: the sexual politics of neoliberalism, in R Castronovo, D Nelson and D Pease (eds), *Materializing Democracy: Toward a revitalized cultural politics*, Duke University Press, New York, pp. 175–94, https://doi.org/10.1515/9780822383901-008 (archived at https://perma.cc/C4UQ-CMGZ)

43 H M Clarke and K A Arnold. Diversity in gender stereotypes? A comparison of heterosexual, gay and lesbian perspectives, *Canadian Journal of Administrative Sciences*, 2017, 34, 149–58, https://doi.org/10.1002/cjas.1437 (archived at https://perma.cc/9XKD-7U3Y)

44 M Brambilla, A Carnaghi and M Ravenna. Status and cooperation shape lesbian stereotypes: testing predictions from the stereotype content mode, *Social Psychology*, 2011, 42 (2), 101–10

45 E Clausell and S T Fiske. When do subgroup parts add up to the stereotypic whole? Mixed stereotype content for gay male subgroups explains overall ratings, *Social Cognition*, 2005, 23 (2), 161–81

46 M Brambilla, A Carnaghi and M Ravenna. Status and cooperation shape lesbian stereotypes: testing predictions from the stereotype content mode, *Social Psychology*, 2011, 42(2), 101–10

47 B E Liberman and F D Golom. Think manager, think male? Heterosexuals' stereotypes of gay and lesbian managers, *Equality, Diversity and Inclusion: An International Journal*, 2015, 34 (7), 566–78

48 J W Morton. Think leader, think heterosexual male? The perceived leadership effectiveness of gay male leaders. *Canadian Journal of Administrative Sciences*, 2017, 34 (2), 159–69, https://doi.org/10.1002/cjas.1434 (archived at https://perma.cc/9XKD-7U3Y)

49 T D Mize and B Manago. The stereotype content of sexual orientation, *Social Currents*, 2018, 5 (5), 458–78, https://doi.org/10.1177/2329496518761999 (archived at https://perma.cc/VH67-8Z2K)

50 S Monro (2015) *Bisexuality: Identities, Politics, and Theories*, Palgrave MacMillan, Basingstoke, England

51 S B Gazzola and M A Morrison. Cultural and personally endorsed stereotypes of transgender men and transgender women: notable correspondence or disjunction?, *International Journal of Transgenderism*, 2014, 15 (2),

76–99, https://doi.org/10.1080/15532739.2014.937041 (archived at https://perma.cc/3U4G-YCKP)

52 Ibid.

53 K Howansky, L Wilton, D Young, S Abrams and R Clapham. (Trans)gender stereotypes and the self: content and consequences of gender identity stereotypes, *Self and Identity*, 2019 20, 1–18, doi:10.1080/15298868.2019.1617191 (archived at https://perma.cc/TUU5-5FPA)

54 C Griggs (1998) *S/he: Changing sex and changing clothes*, Berg, New York

55 K Schilt and C Connell. Do workplace gender transitions make gender trouble? *Gender, Work and Organization*, 2007, 14 (6), 596–618, https://doi.org/10.1111/j.1468-0432.2007.00373.x (archived at https://perma.cc/RLG7-CZHZ)

3

The old boys (white, straight) network and how it affects who gets on

Talent management writers – practitioners more than academics – enjoy using sport and warfare as metaphors. The idea is to show how talent is identified, developed and motivated to perform in situations that are competitive, exciting and high-stakes. The stories are vivid, emotional and public as they often refer to events or characters that we are aware of. They also help establish the credentials of the writer as being of the people, someone that we can relate to.

Metaphors are important because comparing one thing with another helps us to understand concepts with which we are unfamiliar or are complex. This type of metaphor, known as a structural metaphor,[1] can also provide insights on everyday experiences that we may not have considered before. Shakespeare's 'All the world's a stage' is a good example, comparing life to theatre.

Sports metaphors show us how talented athletes make a difference, the importance of creating a team identity and a sense of cohesion. They demonstrate how important it is to ensure that your top performers, the A players, are remunerated more than your B players. They underscore the importance of moving on the poor performers, the C players, and replacing them with others more skilled. To be competitive and successful requires rigorous measuring of performance, reviewing results and implementing change to be ready for the new season. It requires analysis of the competition (the enemy), developing strategy and then ruthless implementation of the plans.

Metaphors, however, are selective, they're not intended to give you the details of a particular situation, but to leave us with an impression of what was done and to suggest what we should be doing. Wouldn't it be great if businesses were like sports teams? Instead of having to make people redundant, we would just sell them instead. Imagine finding someone who is prepared to pay you for the people you wish to offload.

The management authors who I feel can write about sports and warfare with authenticity and legitimacy are those who were themselves professional athletes or soldiers, for example the former NBA basketball player John Amaechi, and former UK table tennis champion Matthew Syed. Whereas the non-athletic talent writers place their attention on the players on the pitch and the inspirational coach that led them, Amaechi and Syed recognize the importance of the many other factors that make a team or individual successful.

In an astonishing opening to his book *Bounce*,[2] Syed recounts his considerable sporting accomplishments, the first line of which reads, 'In January 1995, I became the British number one table tennis player for the very first time which, I am sure you will agree, is a heck of an achievement.' It read like an extended, if justified, brag.

Over the succeeding pages he proceeded to undermine what he had just written about himself. Everything that he had just taken the credit for owed much to the people around him including family, coaches, mentors and an environment that enabled him to flourish. The argument he proposes is that all of these factors were as important to his success, if not more so, than his ability. 'Practically every man or woman who triumphs against the odds is, on closer inspection, a beneficiary of unusual circumstances. The delusion lies in focusing on the individuality of their triumph without perceiving – or bothering to look for – the powerful opportunities stacked in their favour.'[3]

The sporting and military metaphors also send other implied messages:

- It is the individual who is to be acclaimed as the hero of the story.
- It's a zero sum game where in order for you to succeed someone else has to lose.
- Aggression, competitiveness and dominance are the most prized qualities.
- Almost without exception, it is men who are being exalted.
- It plays to the sports 'jock' stereotype of men of being macho and homophobic.[4]

They are also examples of 'greedy institutions',[5] a term coined in the 1970s describing monastic and military organizations that expect you to give body and soul to them, and we can add professional sports teams to that list. They require total devotion and dedication, so any form of flexible working would seem to be an indication of a lack of motivation (this is, remember 'dishonourable' work).

The metaphors used give us an idea about the underlying beliefs that such authors have about talent and the masculine nature of leadership. It is the same reason why CEOs say that their favourite book is the ancient Chinese text *The Art of War*.[6] The book establishes their macho credentials whilst at the same time their cultural and intellectual qualities. (And the best thing about using this book as a reference is that they don't actually have to have read it.)

In this chapter I want to explore some of the other factors, apart from individual talent, which contribute to:

- people's sense of identity and belonging in the workplace
- the support that they receive
- their performance
- being recognized as 'talent'

Identity and belonging

A significant turning point in human evolution took place 12,000 years ago with the advent of agriculture. After that we stopped roaming the landscape and created settlements. Here's a question for you: if human evolution was characterized as an hour, how much time would be represented by the last 12,000 years?

The answer, according to the Dutch evolutionary psychologist Professor Mark van Vugt and his co-author, Ronald Giphart, in their book *Mismatch*, is just 17 seconds.[7] The way we live today has been shaped by events that took place relatively recently, at least in evolutionary terms. The period from the Pleistocene, or Stone Age, to the development of agriculture is several million years. The point that van Vugt and Giphart make is that our brains react in ways that can surprise us, as the subtitle to the book describes: 'How our Stone Age brain deceives us every day [and what we can do about it]'.

Our ancestors lived and worked in stable groups or tribes. Being part of a tribe was essential for one's survival and so we came to learn the signals that showed us that we belonged and were safe with a particular group. By the same token, we also came to spot the signs that told us the opposite. Some of these signals are very subtle indeed and our rational side can tell us that we are overreacting. However, this approach totally ignores our evolutionary inheritance.

Evolutionary psychology provides an important backdrop to our need to identify with and feel part of a group. Social psychology shows how these processes work in practice, and one of the most influential pieces of work is known as social identity theory (SIT) developed by Henri Tajfel and John Turner. They discovered that the behaviour of people changed quite dramatically when they learned which group they were a part of. For example, asked to distribute rewards to people, they responded more favourably to those who were members of the same group, even if they were only recently placed together.

What was most important wasn't maximizing rewards for individuals or collectively but to ensure as big a difference as possible between their group and the others. Satisfaction was achieved by knowing that their group had benefited over another. This effect and desire is so powerful that it was observed even when people had no direct contact with the other members of the group. Fairness was a consideration but mainly to ensure that other members of their group were equitably treated; it did not extend to ensuring fair treatment between the groups. What was more important was that their group could be seen as being better than the other, and this would naturally lead to showing favouritism to their in group members as well as discriminating against out groups.[8]

(Applying this to organizations, this is one of the reasons why paying bonuses to people for hiring 'diverse' candidates does not work in the long run: in-group favouritism will win out over extra remuneration. Failure to understand this is part of the reason why organizations don't achieve the change that they were hoping for merely by providing greater financial incentives.)

Social identity theory breaks down the formation of an identity into three essential stages: categorization, identification and comparison. Categorization is a way of simplifying a very complex world to the barest set of information which enables us to put people into boxes very conveniently. It emphasizes the difference between groups. Stereotypes are an important part of this process; they enable us to make decisions about people very quickly but at the expense of accuracy. The judgments we reach quickly will be very unreliable.

The second step is identification. We, of course, have many different identities and each one will come to the fore when it is most relevant. Our professional identity is most relevant in work contexts, but will be far less relevant when socializing with friends and family where the identity of a parent, sibling, partner or neighbour will be the ones that are most salient. There will be occasions were the identities clash, for example being of the LGBTQ+ community but also part of a religious or ethnic group which is not accepting of that identity. In the workplace, where it is often expected that people will socialize after work, there may be a conflict between the identities of a colleague and parent. The individual has to make a decision in that particular situation as to which identity will take precedence.

Finally, in the third stage we compare groups to which we belong with others and we look for ways in which we are superior to them. This helps to reinforce our identity as well as our self-esteem. Our identity isn't something that we create on our own, in isolation of all others. It is the process of interacting with other people, learning the categories that exist in society, that helps us to form a view of ourselves. We take this with us into our workplaces where this process of social identity is of course being reinforced and replicated.

This has a crucial impact on the way that we behave and think about one another. When a leader is dealing with their team, the subordinates will fall into one of two categories: in groups and out groups, and the relationships formed will be different[9] (see Table 3.1).

There is nothing overtly offensive or discriminatory in the leader's behaviour towards the in group and the out group. Instead it's the subtle behaviours, the nuances, the small gestures of encouragement for some and the absence of them for others that are more common and most telling. Imagine a brief interaction between the leader and an in group team member at the end of each week. One week the leader might say 'great work this week'; at the end of the following week, 'keep it up'; and the week after 'you're doing well'. The interaction lasts barely a second and by the end of the year will have amounted to less than a minute in terms of positive interaction with that team member. That may be all it takes for one person to feel confident, supported and nurtured. It's not that anything negative has happened to the out group member, they just haven't received these affirmations. And of course the in group member will have received

TABLE 3.1 Leader's relationships within group and out group members

In group members	Out group members
High-quality relationship with the leader	Low-quality relationship with the leader
Able to negotiate roles	Little ability to negotiate roles
Leaders don't resort to authority or power to lead	Leader relies on power and authority to influence
Likely to stay	Increased turnover
See themselves as important in the exchange of information, knowledge and support	Relationship is contractual and transactional
Leaders initiate discussions with them	Leaders seldom talk to them
Timely and helpful discussion of performance	Little discussion about effectiveness
Provide tacit support	Little help with difficult work
Discuss personal matters	Discussions rarely move beyond work

other positive signals that they are valued and their contributions recognized by the leader.

I was explaining to a group of senior managers in a client meeting about in groups and out groups. One of the people said he found it very interesting but he was pleased to report that there were no in groups and out groups in his organization. A rule of thumb, if anybody ever says there are no in groups and out groups where they work, they are in the in group.

One of the privileges of being in the in group is that you don't have to recognize or worry about the fact that there are divisions in the team. If you are in the out group you are well aware that there are things going on that you are not party to, such as receiving information, being connected with others in the organization and receiving advice from the leader. The recipient of the extra time, guidance and support won't necessarily be aware of the advantages that they have, assuming that other team members have the same open relationship with the leader. As Matthew Syed observed, we are often unaware of the factors in our environment that are supporting the development of our skills, ambitions and self-belief.

Feeling like an outsider within your team can also be detected by small behaviours. Imagine someone coming to a busy office on a Monday morning. The receptionist greets them with a cheery smile; on entering the crowded lift they notice someone pressed up against the back wall and they exchange a roll of the eyes and another smile as if to say 'the start of another week'; walking into the office, the boss is already there on a video conference call and waves hello; and while waiting for the computer to boot up they go for the first of several shots of caffeine that will sustain them through the day and engage in a conversation with colleagues about what they were up to over the weekend. Nothing unusual or untoward here, and on the surface it all looks pretty mundane; yet everything that happened demonstrates to that individual that this is a place where they belong. Now imagine someone else arriving in the same office building at the same time and receiving none of these affirmations. Or worse, they are behind the person who has been so warmly received and so make a comparison.

As evolutionary psychologists have informed us, we are very sensitive to the cues that tell us whether we belong or not, whether we are in the in group or not.

Micro-incivilities

The workplace is not just the absence of welcoming behaviours, there are also behaviours that can make people feel uncomfortable. The term 'microaggressions' is one that is now commonly used since being popularized in the book *Microaggressions in Everyday Life* by Derald Wing Sue.[10] I have a slight difficulty with the word microaggression. It's generally accepted that because the behaviours we are talking about are so small people may not be aware that they are making others feel uncomfortable and excluded. By choosing to describe it as a form of 'aggression' it eliminates the possibility that it could have been carried out unconsciously. There are a lot of people who don't have a problem with that, because they are of the opinion that these acts could never have been carried out without the person's awareness. When acts of discrimination or prejudice take place there are usually three principal actors: victims, perpetrators and bystanders. People accept that they could be victims, that they almost certainly will be bystanders, but they could never imagine themselves being the perpetrators. These are the people who don't believe such actions could be carried out unconsciously. The result is that as the perpetrator engaged in this behaviour deliberately they will need to be punished. However, the fact of the matter is that we could all find ourselves in any one of those three roles, including perpetrator. Those who believe there is no such thing as unconscious bias, when accused of being a perpetrator, to remain consistent with their beliefs, will never be able to claim that they acted with a lack of awareness and that they did not realize what they did.

There is also research that has identified that pro-social behaviours lend themselves both to employee satisfaction and organizational performance. These are referred to as organizational citizenship behaviours, the term first being coined by researchers Thomas Bateman and Dennis Organ.[11] Civil behaviour, essentially showing respect towards one another, has come to be seen as important in the workplace for productive relationships. Incivility came to be seen as being something destructive in the workplace, worthy of attention itself. Workplace civility is seen as behaviours 'involving politeness and regard for others in the workplace, within workplace norms for respect'. Workplace incivility, essentially an antonym of workplace civility, is defined as 'acting with disregard for others in the workplace, in violation of workplace norms for respect'.[12]

My preference is to use the concepts that have already been developed and applied to the workplace and to think of the small behaviours as being micro-incivilities, which I define as 'the kinds of daily, commonplace behaviours or aspects of an environment which signal, wittingly or unwittingly, to members of out groups that they do not belong and are not welcome'.[13] This approach builds on the well-established organizational citizenship behaviour work and allows for the possibility that individuals may engage in such behaviour without being aware that they're doing it.

The types of micro-incivilities that people experience will depend on the group to which they are seen to belong. If women are in the out group they are less likely to have their ideas discussed within the team. I have lost count of the number of occasions that women have told me about their frustration at making a suggestion and it being met with silence, only for a man to be complimented for making the same suggestion a few minutes later. Women have also reported feeling frustrated at being mistaken for being in a support role rather than the leader, or being asked to make the coffee and so emphasizing their subservient role within the team.

I was once presenting the results of a gender audit that I had been asked to carry out for the European operations of a US internet company. The organization was young, as they all are, and full of younger people who saw themselves as liberal, open minded and tolerant. In the focus groups I conducted, in particular the female-only ones, it was clear that many women felt excluded and underappreciated at work. One observation that was made by women in every location was that many of the informal conversations that took place at work were based around football and Formula One racing. As many of the women were not interested in these sports they didn't participate and consequently they didn't have the opportunity to form connections with the men.

There were lots of other things reported back to the senior management team, but the European HR director decided to test out this one observation. At the next meeting with a group of senior colleagues she noticed that they were talking about football. Ordinarily she would not have joined in but on this occasion she did and talked about her passion for Chelsea Football Club and the results over the weekend. To her surprise not only did the men not engage with her, the conversation was changed to discuss rugby. She is also a fan of rugby so engaged enthusiastically about the international rugby results. Perplexed, the conversation took another turn, this time to discuss cricket, which is a sport that she also follows as she lives not far from Lord's cricket ground. She had much pleasure recounting the incident to me but also emphasized that these conversations, whether people realize it or not, are designed to enable the in group to bond to the exclusion of others. These conversations are driven by the expectation that some people will be drawn into them and others will be left out.

Racial micro-incivilities also have their own special character. I was once asked by a very senior academic at a prestigious university why it was wrong, as she had been told, to ask someone from a visible minority the question 'Where are you from?' In fact, there is nothing wrong with that question, it's the one that follows it that is problematic: 'No, where are you really from?' The questioner is assuming that people of colour must be immigrants to the country. Racial incivilities also include constantly mispronouncing somebody's name – minority group members can tell the difference when somebody is genuinely making an effort to pronounce the name correctly, and when people cannot be bothered.

One Sunday evening I received a text from a friend who worked as a senior correspondent in a UK broadcast organization asking whether it was a problem that her boss, the editor of the news show, constantly referred to her by the name of the other Asian woman in the department. I replied saying it was a problem. This is a journalist who was well known and publicly recognizable. It was a travesty that her own boss couldn't distinguish her from the other brown person in her team, and she was in effect saying that 'I don't think you're anywhere near as important as you think you are'. You won't be surprised to learn that, despite working for this organization for many years, she decided to leave for a more prestigious job at a much more senior level.

The assumption that a disabled person requires assistance and help is something that is frequently experienced, particularly by those who are wheelchair users.

In addition, there is also something referred to as the spread phenomenon. The term was coined by Beatrice Wright who described it as follows:

> If a person who was below standard in one characteristic felt inferior
> only in that regard and not in general, his feelings of inadequacy
> would not be destructive of the personality… Unfortunately, so sane
> an appraisal of personal liabilities is not the rule. Physique (as well as
> certain other personal characteristics) has an enormous power to evoke
> a wide variety of impressions and feelings about the person. In fact,
> physical deviation is frequently seen as the central key to a person's
> behavior and personality and largely responsible for the important
> ramifications in the person's life.[14]

It's a wonderful description because it shows how when we know about a person's disability it spreads to affect our judgement about them on aspects of their personality and competence which are totally unrelated.

Other examples include being infantilized and being seen to be inadequate to undertake tasks that other people can do or being overpraised for doing fairly routine tasks.

Micro-incivilities experienced by the LGBTQ+ community include heteronormative assumptions being made about an individual, for example taking it for granted that somebody will be straight. It also extends to expectations of what the sex of someone's partner will be. Again one-off occurrences like this are not necessarily problematic, but when repeated several times it becomes frustrating and tiring.

Homophobic language is obviously an issue but there are also expressions which have become more popular to express disapproval of something ('that's so gay'). Other examples include repeatedly using the wrong pronouns for somebody. The additional stress that acts like these may cause is due to the fact that being LGBTQ+ is an invisible identity and not one that has necessarily been shared with colleagues at work. Hearing homophobic comments or jokes creates additional pressure and conflict for a person who has not come out, as they have to decide whether to challenge the remark or to remain silent.

Here's an interesting fact for you: of all the primates we are the only ones who have sclera, otherwise known as the white of our eyes.[15] Because of this we are able to look at things by just moving our eyes, whereas all other primates have to move their head in the direction they wish to look. Eye contact is very important to us and you can see this in the behaviour of babies with their parents. They learn quickly to first look into the eyes and face of the parent, and then later they are able to follow the gaze of the adult to see what they are looking at. Eye contact also transmits emotion – there are countless love songs referring to looking into one's partner's eyes. A micro-incivility experienced by many out groups is being denied eye contact by team members and/or the leader. The individuals concerned may not be aware that they're doing it and others who are present may not realise this is happening but one thing you can be sure of is that the person on the receiving end of it will know it's going on. Because it seems so insignificant, people experiencing this will have difficulty knowing how to respond. Furthermore there is ambiguity in the situation because they will not be sure whether this is happening deliberately or even whether it's happening at all. When this occurs on a regular basis it leads to people experiencing not only discomfort and frustration, but feeling stressed about how they should deal with it. After reading my work on micro-incivilities, an Asian head of department in a school decided to tell her colleague, the school's deputy head, let's call him Tom, that the head of the school never looked at her in meetings and she inquired whether he had ever noticed that. His reply was 'Why would I?' Tom's dismissive response made it clear that he saw this as an insignificant issue and there were bigger problems to be dealing with. If you've never been on the receiving end of behaviour like that you won't know what it feels like. Yet it is exactly behaviours like this that evolutionary psychologists have identified as giving us the clues as to whether we belong in a group or not.

Impact of being excluded

The effect of all of this is ultimately, from the organization's perspective, a negative impact on performance. Psychologist Jonathan Taylor describes how this happens through four factors[16] (see Figure 3.1):

1 Physiological impairment. The stress hormone, cortisol, is released in response to the behaviour of others. Amongst other things this leads to an increased heart rate and higher blood pressure as well as affecting the functioning of the prefrontal cortex of the brain, which impacts our decision making.

2 Monitoring of ourselves and others. Once we have had experience of being excluded in a group we start to monitor other environments to identify whether this could be happening again. It can make us more sensitive to the actions of others.

3 Task-related thoughts and worries. Instead of being able to concentrate on their work, people will become overly concerned about the perception of other people to what they're doing, in effect second-guessing themselves.

4 Suppression of thoughts. People become aware of the extraneous thoughts that they're having and will attempt to suppress them. Ironically this places an extra burden on their working memory.

The impact on performance is most likely to be more visible in more complex tasks, the ones where focus and concentration are needed. These are also the tasks that can get people noticed if successfully carried out and can help to earmark people as having the potential to progress.

This will impact people's self-confidence, and one way in which this shows itself is through individuals not seeking out support from others around them. This not only means that they are less likely to obtain advice and guidance helpful to them, but also that they are less likely to develop relationships with others.[17]

In a major review of the literature it was found that supportive colleagues had the greatest impact on people's wellbeing, engagement and sense of purpose.[18] This research was carried out on LGBTQ+ employees but the results will be applicable to other groups too.

FIGURE 3.1 Impact of identity threat

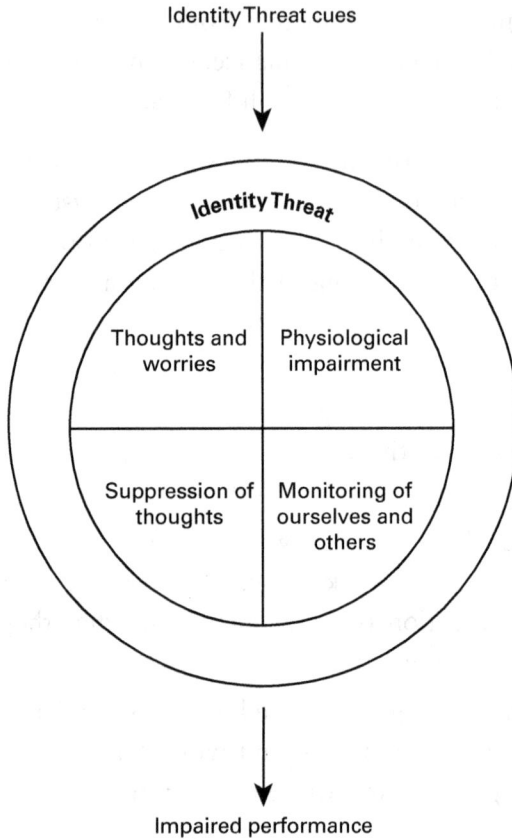

Networks

When people talk about meritocracy at work there is an underlying belief that hard work, effective performance and compliance with organizational values will be noticed irrespective of your background.

The highly respected business anthropologist Fred Luthans decided to see whether this was in fact the case. He looked at the range of tasks that managers carried out, including working with one's team and externally oriented activities such as communicating with their boss as well as people in other departments. He looked at those managers who were seen as the most effective as well as those who were seen as the most successful, defined as those who were promoted more quickly than others.

You might have expected a relationship between the two, in that the most effective managers were the ones who were promoted more quickly. In fact he found that they were quite different. The most effective managers actually spent more time working with their teams: clarifying objectives, creating plans, providing support, coaching and monitoring performance. The ones who were more successful spent the majority of their time networking with others outside of their teams.

So whilst we like to believe we use performance data to evaluate whether somebody has the potential to progress, Luthans demonstrated that it was nothing of the sort. Self-promotion, assiduous relationship building and networking were the keys to being promoted and identified as having potential.

Being part of a dominant network in an organization is key to being promoted, and being excluded from these has a significant effect on your promotion prospects.

Networks can be examined using a number of criteria: homophily, density, cohesiveness and multiplexity.

Homophily theory was first outlined in 1954 by the sociologists and long-time collaborators Paul F Lazarsfeld and Robert K. Merton in their study of friendship in two US towns.[19] Essentially communication between two people is easier when they are more alike to one another. They will share the same perspectives on the world, use the same language and have the same frames of reference. When they are exchanging information or views therefore it will be done very efficiently with little additional explanation needed because they know where the other one is coming from. The disadvantage, of course, is that they will not be exposed to people who hold different views and perspectives on the world.

The same thing occurs within organizations where the most powerful networks, the ones that help to advance people's careers, tend to exclude people who are different from the majority of people in them. This is what people are talking about when they refer to 'the old boys network'. The vagueness with which people refer to this often leads to the very notion being dismissed. Social network analysis, however, has provided a methodology which enables us to create powerful pictures of the ways in which people relate to one another in the workplace. Visual differences can be a reason to exclude people from a network, for example on the grounds of gender[20] and ethnicity[21] because it will be assumed they have little in common with the rest of the group. Out group members have to work harder to be noticed; for example, disabled people have to engage in more ingratiating behaviour with their line manager in order to achieve higher performance ratings.[22]

Density reflects the strength of the ties between people in a group. The greater the connection between all people in the group, the higher the density. Myself and a colleague were carrying out a team review in a group of 30 people in a major law firm, examining how they were working together, and trying to find out why they were experiencing difficulties. As part of the process we carried out a network analysis: 33 per cent (10) of the people in the group were women which, given the seniority of the group, was a high proportion compared to other teams.

The analysis showed that this group was split into two, with a very dense inner network with the leader at its heart and an outer group that was far less connected. We also found that 9 out of the 10 women were in the outer group. Therefore the relationships in this very senior group of people were gendered. Being in the in group has distinct advantages because it provides access to information, resources and opportunities.

At the time, we were surprised at the reaction of the group who didn't immediately want to discuss this any further. At a later point, however, they were in a better frame of mind to be able to reflect on this and also to discuss how relationships could be strengthened within the team. Greater density within a team also enables greater fairness because people are much more aware of how other people are being treated and paid, for example. In the 19th century factory owners soon learned that one of the ways to pay women less than men for the same job was to have them working on different floors of the building. Networks keep in group and out group members separated from one another in a much more subtle way.

Multiplexity is the extent to which the same people are involved in different networks. Where individuals are working together and socializing together the networks will have people in both of them. Where in group and out group patterns are reflected in out-of-work socialization it creates the conditions for favouritism if not cronyism to occur. In work we have carried out, women will often say that they are unable to take part in out-of-work socializing because they have caring and domestic responsibilities. Minorities can find a drinking culture conflicts with their own personal and cultural habits. Members of the LGBTQ+ community who have not come out at work will avoid social events partly because they will not wish to inadvertently reveal their sexual orientation to colleagues.

Cohesiveness is a reflection of the emotions that people feel towards one another. In a cohesive group people will feel that they want to stay in touch with one another because of the strength of the emotional connection between them. The relationships and the network will remain intact for a longer period of time. It also helps in building a career. While talent management writers enjoy using sports as a metaphor, the focus is almost entirely on the athletes and the head coach. It never extends to looking at the nature of the organization that sits behind a team. Approximately 25 per cent of footballers playing in the English Premier League are from minorities, the majority being black. Being a footballer, no matter how successful, is only one of the jobs that is available to someone if they want to work in the industry.

Head coaches, and indeed coaches at lower levels in any club, will tend to have been professional footballers. The number of black players who successfully transitioned into management is ridiculously small, despite having gained the professional qualifications.[23] Analysis we carried out revealed that black players were half as likely to be captains as white players.[24] Or to put it another way, black players were not seen as having leadership qualities to captain the team on the pitch. Captaincy meant meeting senior officials and others in the club, who became part of their network. Knowing the chairman and other directors of the club provided management and coaching opportunities, where further links and connections were made. It is sometimes mystifying to fans how some people, irrespective of the results they have achieved, continue to get high level, highly remunerated coaching positions. It is because of the cohesiveness of the networks where people have emotional bonds of trust and respect for one another.

Looking at the appointment of people into coaching positions and improving the selection process is important, but it totally ignores the impact that these informal, not immediately visible networks have in terms of progressing one's career in that industry. Where talent writers focus on the performers only, they are asking us to draw lessons about leadership based on what are essentially entry-level jobs, something that they would never do when providing observations on other sectors.

Key points

It isn't possible to separate out performance from socialization in the workplace. Social identity theory shows how people can be separated into in groups and out groups with surprising speed. Observable differences enable this to happen very quickly, for example on the grounds of gender, ethnicity and where someone has a visible disability. Where an identity is not immediately evident, for example one's sexual orientation or a disability that is not apparent, individuals may choose not to reveal this to their colleagues because they are well aware of the possible stigmatization they may experience should they do so.

Being in the in group has considerable positive consequences, most notably that they don't have to consider whether they are part of a privileged group at all. They can be more themselves, more authentic, in the workplace. Out group members will be aware of being excluded, which has consequences in terms of physiological, behavioural and emotional responses. They will be aware of the often small signals that are sent that show them that they don't belong to this group. These may seem trivial, particularly to in group members who are not subject to these behaviours on a regular basis, but evolutionary psychology shows us that they are critically important. It's an essential part of being human that we want to belong to a group or, as evolutionary psychologists would put it, to a tribe. Innately, and the latest neuroscience research demonstrates this, we can interpret the signals being sent to us which show us whether we are part of a group or not.

I find it incredibly compelling that if human evolution was characterized as an hour, the last 12,000 years would represent only 17 seconds.

The sense of inclusion or exclusion has an impact on performance. Being excluded leads to poorer performance compared to being included. It also has an impact in terms of networks in organizations. The old boys network has long been described as a mechanism for excluding people from progressing in organizations. Despite our familiarity with the expression, it still remains vague and difficult to articulate. More recent research, however, particularly using social network analysis, has made the relationships between people visible.

We can see that in terms of homophily, density, multiplexity and cohesiveness networks can impede the progression of some people and at the same time propel the careers of others. Ultimately this limits the effectiveness of teams and organizations because the lack of different perspectives means less creativity and innovation. In group favouritism means that we are restricting the number of people in the talent pool because we will not be identifying talent in fair and effective ways.

Notes

1 G Lakoff and M Johnson. The metaphorical structure of the human conceptual system, *Cognitive Science*, 1980, 4 (2), 195–208

2 M Syed and J Clamp (2010) *Bounce*, HarperCollins, London, p. 3

3 Ibid, p. 9

4 E Anderson and M McCormack. Inclusive masculinity theory: overview, reflection and refinement, *Journal of Gender Studies*, 2018, 27 (5), 547–61

5 L A Coser (1974) *Greedy Institutions: Patterns of undivided commitment*, Collier Macmillan, New York

6 G Beyer. Why business leaders are obsessed with Sun Tzu's ancient military guide, "The Art of War", HuffPost, 24 March 2014, www.huffingtonpost.co.uk/entry/why-business-leaders-are_n_5003283 (archived at https://perma.cc/9FTH-HF59)

7 R Giphart and M Van Vugt (2018) *Mismatch: How our stone age brain deceives us every day (and what we can do about it)*, Robinson

8 H Tajfel and J C Turner (1979) An integrative theory of intergroup conflict, in W G Austin, and S Worchel (eds), *The Social Psychology of Intergroup Relations*, Brooks/Cole, Monterey, CA, pp. 33–37

9 F J Landy and J M Conte (2009) *Work in the 21st Century–An introduction to industrial and organizational psychology*, 3rd edn, John Wiley, New York

10 D W Sue (2009) *Microaggressions in Everyday Life: Race, gender and sexual orientation*, John Wiley, New York

11 T S Bateman and D W Organ. Job satisfaction and the good soldier: the relationship between affect and employee 'citizenship', *Academy of Management Journal*, 1983, 26 (4), 587–95

12 L M Andersson and C M Pearson. Tit for tat? The spiraling effect of incivility in the workplace, *Academy of Management Review*, 1999 24 (3), 452–71, pp. 454–55

13 B Kandola (2018) *Racism at Work: The danger of indifference*, Pearn Kandola Publishing, Oxford, p. 101

14 B Wright (1963) *Physical Disability: A psychological approach*, Harper & Row, New York, p. 118

15 R Giphart and M Van Vugt (2018) *Mismatch: How our stone age brain deceives us every day (and what we can do about it)*, Robinson

16 J Taylor (2020) *How Discrimination Affects Our Performance in Free to Soar: Race and well-being in organisations*, Pearn Kandola Publishing, Oxford

17 S E Martiny and J Nikitin. Social identity threat in interpersonal relationships: activating negative stereotypes decreases social approach motivation, *Journal of Experimental Psychology: Applied*, 2019, 25 (1), 117

18 J R Webster, G A Adams, C L Maranto, K Sawyer and C Thoroughgood. Workplace contextual supports for LGBT employees: a review, meta-analysis, and agenda for future research, *Human Resource Management*, 2018, 57 (1), 193–210

19 P F Lazarsfeld and R K Merton (1954) Friendship as a social process: a substantive and methodological analysis, in M Berger (ed), *Freedom and Control in Modern Society*, Van Nostrand, New York, 18–66

20 H Ibarra. Homophily and differential returns: sex differences in network structure and access in an advertising firm, *Administrative Science Quarterly*, 1992, 422–47

21 A Mehra, M Kilduff and D J Brass. At the margins: a distinctiveness approach to the social identity and social networks of underrepresented groups, *Academy of Management Journal*, 1998, 41 (4), 441–52

22 A Colella and A Varma. The impact of subordinate disability on leader-member exchange relationships, *Academy of Management Journal*, 2001, 44 (2), 304–15

23 House of Commons Culture, Media and Sport Committee (2012) *Racism in Football: Second Report of Session 2012–13*, The Stationary Office Ltd, London

24 B Kandola (2018) *Racism at Work: The danger of indifference*, Pearn Kandola Publishing, Oxford

4

Attracting and selecting talent

Ask a local in any city the best places to eat and they will usually ask you the type of cuisine you're looking for, as the answer will direct you to different districts. Indian food? It's the Balti Triangle you will want. Chinese? Head for Chinatown. Italian? Little Italy is the place to go. We recognize that separate ethnic communities are more likely to be found in some parts of the city than others. Fascinating and beautiful maps of the ethnic make-up of the United Kingdom have been produced by the Office for National Statistics in the UK and they show where different ethnic communities are more likely to be congregated.[1] Does that mean that people living in those communities have an innate desire to live separately from others? Does the choice of where people want to live reveal racial prejudice? It was questions such as these that Thomas Schelling set out to answer when he looked closely at community segregation in the US.[2]

Schelling's famous experiment on community segregation starts with a surprisingly simple and clever idea: tiny, everyday preferences can lead to surprisingly big social outcomes. Here's how it works.

Imagine a chessboard where each square is a home. You place some red and blue coins on the board to represent people of two different groups – let's say these represent different ethnicities or backgrounds. Schelling asked a simple question: What happens if each person wants to live near some of their own group but doesn't mind having a few neighbours from the other group?

To simulate this, he set a small rule: if more than a third of someone's neighbours are from the other group, they would want to move to a different spot on the board. So, you start moving coins around to places where they'd feel more comfortable, repeating the process over and over.

What Schelling discovered was fascinating: even though no one had an extreme preference for segregation, small preferences caused a ripple effect. Over time, the coins naturally clustered into entirely segregated areas, with reds on one side and blues on the other.

This elegant experiment led to Schelling's famous model of segregation, showing how even mild personal preferences can unintentionally create larger patterns of division in communities. The key takeaway (pun intended): sometimes, segregation happens not because people want it, but because small, seemingly harmless choices add up over time to create major social patterns. Once groups become separated like this it's easy to see how one group can view themselves very differently to another, stereotyping them and viewing them as inferior. Yet the differentiation that occurred was based on very little bias at all. So small biases can lead to a much bigger impact when decisions are made.

Recent studies have identified the same effects occurring in the selection process, with the title of one paper telling us all we need to know: 'Small biases in hiring evaluations have big consequences'.[3] Whilst Schelling's work is not directly acknowledged, the study by Jay H Hardy III and his colleagues is a demonstration, in a different context, of the earlier work. In this study a literature review was conducted first to identify the types and magnitude of biases that occur during the selection process. The puzzle for them was that many of the biases appeared to be relatively small, which was something they were determined to investigate in more depth.

Using the power of technology unimaginable in the 1960s when Schelling conducted his research, Hardy and the team used computer simulations to model the effects of small biases in hiring. These simulations provided a powerful way to explore long-term outcomes across multiple hiring cycles, capturing how biases could accumulate and alter the demographic composition of an organization.

The simulations began by assuming a slight bias in hiring evaluations, such as a minor preference for male candidates. The biases modelled were small, representing slight tendencies rather than overt discrimination. The researchers simulated repeated hiring cycles, allowing them to observe how these small biases played out over time.

To simulate the hiring process, the researchers inputted various factors such as qualifications, performance metrics and various degrees of gender bias. They then tracked how these biases affected the likelihood of different candidates being hired, even when their qualifications were identical or nearly identical. Over many rounds of simulated hiring, the model revealed how small preferences for certain groups could lead to substantial differences in representation.

The key innovation of this study was using computer modelling to visualize how minor biases could result in large, systemic inequalities in organizational composition. When specific selection processes are examined it is not possible to see the longer-term impact of aggregated decision. By simulating multiple hiring cycles, the researchers could observe the compounding effect of these small biases and their potential to skew the overall workforce diversity in an organization. They also looked at the impact of the decisions on something they refer to as NHFR, the new hire failure rate.

The findings from the computer simulations were both revealing and alarming. Even when the biases in favour of men were extremely small – sometimes as little as a 1–2 per cent preference – the cumulative effect over time was dramatic. Across many hiring cycles, these small biases could lead to significant overrepresentation of this group especially at more senior levels.

For example, in scenarios where men were slightly preferred over women for a position, the simulations showed that after many rounds of hiring, the organization would become overwhelmingly male, even though the qualifications of male and female candidates were similar. This happens because small biases, when applied consistently over time, build up and amplify. Imagine setting off on a journey and being slightly off track at the beginning. As you progress the variation between where you should be and where you are grows – and that's what's happening here. As a result, women are gradually removed from consideration, despite being equally qualified.

In organizations, even minor biases in performance evaluations or selection decisions could lead to major underrepresentation of certain groups, creating workplace cultures that are less diverse and more homogeneous than intended.

The authors concluded that while each individual decision might be influenced by only a marginal bias, the cumulative impact over time can drastically reduce the presence of women and, to extend their finding, to minorities, and other underrepresented groups in an organization. In a different context, this was the same conclusion that Schelling reached.

The key lesson to be learned is the importance of addressing even these small biases to prevent large-scale inequalities from emerging. Organizations must recognize and be vigilant about the potential for these biases to accumulate and take proactive measures to mitigate them. This could involve implementing standardized hiring processes, structured evaluation criteria and regular diversity audits to ensure that biases are not creeping into decisions.

Attraction

It's also important to bear in mind that bias, this time within society, will have had an impact in terms of who is attracted to certain roles and particular organizations.

Some talent management theorists have put forward the view that people find jobs that suit their personality. That's probably true for white straight men but doesn't necessarily apply to groups of people beyond that.

Vocational psychologist Linda Gottfriedson's theory of circumscription and compromise is particularly relevant here when it comes to gender.[4] Personalities play a part in career choice, but they aren't the be-all and end-all. Children inevitably pick up ideas about jobs and roles that are carried out by men and women, and what this means in terms of their own career choices. This is the circumscription part of her theory, where we start to make decisions and choices about which jobs roles are the appropriate or inappropriate ones. In her research she found children as young as six were already formu-lating ideas about the types of job and career that would be attractive to them, based on their gender.

Other factors also come into play, of course, such as how difficult is it to get into a particular profession. Generally speaking, the more high status the profession the fewer women will be found in it. The gender diversity that exists within the profession obviously helps people to determine whether it's one that they should seriously consider.

Career choice therefore is a partly positive process of choosing a sector and role but it's also one of closing doors on certain jobs based on the diversity of people that we see in them. The compromise is then to decide which options to pursue, having given up on others that were felt to be inappropriate and more difficult to attain.

Wouldn't it be wonderful if you could have a personality assess-ment of children at an early age and then follow them up to see what careers and roles they eventually ended up working in? We would then be able to see the relationship between personality, career choice and the impact of other variables such as societal attitudes. Somewhat remarkably this type of study has been carried out.

Between the years 1959 and 1967 on the Hawaiian islands of Oahu and Kauai nearly 2,500 elementary school children had their personalities assessed. Decades later, when the original children were aged between 45 and 55 years of age, 587 of these children were followed up to see what careers they had pursued. Psychologists Steve Woods and Sarah Hampson analysed this data,[5] using the respected RIASEC vocational theory model of vocational types to classify jobs.

Developed by John Holland, RIASEC, also known as Holland's theory of career choice, categorizes individuals and work environ-ments into six personality types: Realistic, Investigative, Artistic, Social, Enterprising and Conventional (RIASEC). Each type reflects specific preferences, behaviours and skills, guiding career interests.

- **Realistic (Doers)** prefer practical, hands-on activities, often in mechanical or outdoor work.

- **Investigative (Thinkers)** are drawn to analytical, intellectual tasks, such as science or research.

- **Artistic (Creators)** favour creative, unstructured activities like writing, art or music.

- **Social (Helpers)** are inclined toward interpersonal work, including teaching or counselling.

- **Enterprising (Persuaders)** seek leadership or entrepreneurial roles that involve persuading or managing others.

- **Conventional (Organizers)** enjoy structured, detail-oriented tasks such as accounting or administration.

Career success and satisfaction are higher when there's a good fit between the individual's type and the job's characteristics. The RIASEC model is widely used in career counselling and education, helping individuals identify career paths that match their strengths, interests and values. It promotes self-understanding and assists in making informed career choices based on personality compatibility. Woods and Hampson found that career choices were a combination of personality and socialization effects.

In later life people were in careers that generally fitted with societal expectations of what men and women should be doing, as opposed to being in professions that suited their personalities. Gender differences were found in the occupational preferences of men and women. Men show greatest interest in Realistic and Investigative roles, while women have greatest interest in Artistic, Social and Conventional which is consistent with the male-female agentic-communal stereotype divide.

The personality dimension of openness, which is related to imagination, curiosity and originality, was most related to individuals working in counter-stereotypical careers. Children who scored high on this dimension had the curiosity to be able to explore counter-stereotypical options further and were able to visualize themselves working in occupations that were not associated with their gender. Boys scoring low on this dimension was predictive of them working in Realistic occupations. Girls scoring low on this dimension was predictive of them working in Conventional occupations.

Societal expectations of what men and women should be doing in their careers has an impact on children and their ambitions. When youngsters have a personality that means they are able to think of themselves in roles that are not associated with their gender, they are more able to go their own way, and to resist the pressures that society places on them. It is important then that we are aware that values and attitudes that children are exposed to have an impact in terms of their careers, which means that even before we have tried to attract people to certain occupations, societal pressures and expectations will already have limited the talent pool that is eventually available to organizations.

I once completed the MBTI as part of a training programme that I was on. Everyone was asked to share their profile with the facilitator and I was a little surprised when I was told, on sharing mine, that I couldn't have completed it correctly. The facilitator was very confident that on one of the dimensions I was the opposite of what the results had shown. I said I used to be like that but that I had to learn to change my approach to make myself more effective in my work. I was told in no uncertain terms that our personalities are stable and unchanging. This is the orthodox view of personality and that being the case it will enable us to make confident predictions about people's behaviour in the future. When it comes to identifying leaders, therefore, they are born and not developed.

Using the same Hawaiian dataset, Woods and Hampson, this time with other colleagues, demonstrated that this isn't necessarily the case at all, and as well as personality traits maturing, they can also change as a result of experiences in our lives including the type of work we do.[6] The sample of people in the study had completed personality questionnaires in their childhood (in 1965 or 1967) and in adulthood (in 2005 and 2013). Using the RIASEC model they were able to see the extent to which people were in occupations that fitted with their personality, and those who were in roles that did not. They found that where there was a fit, known as vocational gravitation, there was a further development of the qualities that attracted them to those occupations in the first place. However, where there was a misfit, individuals adapted their behaviour, and when this was done on a repeated basis these skills and traits became more developed and reinforced. In other words, the environment has an impact in terms of people's personalities, which then enables them to function in that occupation.

Consistent with what they found in the earlier study, those who were high on openness were also those who showed this form of development. It's often the case that when we are trying to fill a role, a selected individual will have gaps in their experience and areas where they do not fill the profile of the ideal person. Woods and the team conclude that we should be looking at those gaps as opportunities rather than limitations and finding ways in which people can be developed further.

A similar pattern of being drawn to certain sectors and organizations, and a rejection of others, can be seen in the employment pattern of members of the LGBTQ+ community. It has long been noticed how people are more likely to be in certain roles and sectors. Bullying and harassment at school means on average a lower level of educational attainment, which then can restrict ambitions. Another consideration for members of the LGBTQ+ community will be safety and the extent to which a person can be themselves in the workplace.

The types of jobs and careers that they will be drawn to are those that enable them to work independently, and the ones generally avoided are those that require greater levels of teamwork. The consequences of being out where people work in relative isolation from one another will be less than if they are part of a cohesive group of people. (It's another reason why the sports and military analogies cannot be universally applied to every group of people.)[7]

As tempting as it is, personal choice based on interests and personalities cannot explain totally how and why people end up in the careers that they have. Failure to look at issues of diversity and inclusion means that we only ever have a partial understanding of how talent pools are created.

It is important, therefore, that professional bodies as well as the bigger organizations themselves strive to expand children's knowledge about what possibilities are available to them. It's important that teachers understand that whilst career choices can be informed by someone's interests, these may be the result of learning about society's attitudes towards the type of roles people should be going into.

It will also be based on experiences that people have had on sharing their identity with others, and, having been stigmatized, the need to work in safe environments will take precedence over having the perfect alignment between one's capabilities and one's job.

The new boys network: The role of executive search

Executive search firms were one of the immediate beneficiaries of McKinsey's alarmist War for Talent.

They quickly came to be seen as an essential ingredient in an organization's talent management programme, and yet somehow they seem to have escaped any significant attention. They have become the gatekeepers to organizations and are the ones who are prominent in defining 'it' (talent management) and stressing its importance, typically emphasizing the risks of getting these appointments wrong.[8] The WFT represented the opportunity they needed to expand their markets and present themselves to their clients as the only people who are able to source talented individuals either nationally or globally. According to the Association of Executive Search Consultants (AESC), between 1978 and the early 2000s their members saw a steady increase in revenues. With growing demand related to the WFT between 2004 and 2008 there was an increase of 120 per cent. Between 2012 and 2019 revenues reached $16 billion, and following the pandemic where there was a slight dip, it rebounded in 2021 to $19.9 billion, and then to $21.1 billion in 2022.[9]

This is a significant industry with an enormous impact which deserves to have its activities more rigorously researched than has been the case.

There are a number of phases that represent the search for an executive position. The first phase involves mapping the market, which is where the researchers and consultants list competing firms where they may be able to find eligible candidates. The process then moves to sourcing the candidates, using a database of suitable people, and finally to obtaining an assessment of them. It's usually the executive search firm which will have the profile of the ideal candidate and who will be the ones to approach the people they think would be a good match. The first approach to an individual will not provide very much information at all, not even about the organization. Part of the reason this is done is that for these very senior executive roles, there is much negotiation that takes place both in terms of remuneration and also the way the job will be structured. Details obviously become firmed up once an offer is finalized.

One thing that consultants have told researchers is that they are wary of executives approaching them looking to move roles, believing this might well cause difficulties for the organization that they might join.[10] Nevertheless, being part of an executive search firm's network is clearly beneficial. When they have contacted you and know about your qualification, credentials and ambitions, you are more likely to discover more suitable opportunities. The search for candidates doesn't start from scratch and whilst the firms present themselves as a meritocratic alternative to the old boys network, it has been labelled as the 'new boys network'.[11]

Speaking from experience, many of our clients are frustrated with the lack of diversity on the shortlists that many executive search firms provide. The firms themselves will say, with some justification, that because there is so little diversity particularly in regard to gender and ethnicity (typically the areas of most interest), it's unreasonable to expect them to produce lists that don't reflect the reality. Research has also shown however that executive search firms show bias in the way they go about sourcing and selecting people.

The decision-making process is conservative as the firms want to have candidates that they are able to defend having on the shortlist. People who have experience at prestigious organizations are the ones who will be favoured, and those who may have the requisite skills but work at organizations deemed to be more run-of-the-mill won't be considered at all. This will exclude people from minority groups, for example, who are more likely to be working in the public and voluntary sectors. They will also favour people who have attended prestigious higher education establishments.

Most of the people who work as consultants in executive search firms are male and white. Typically, they have much less information about female and minority professionals who may not be part of their network. They have been found to have more contacts and greater information about white male candidates.[12] Informal contacts and informal networks carry considerable weight in deciding who will be suitable or not. This becomes problematic for people who are a member of out groups because they won't be part of those informal, but hugely influential, networks.

Executive search firms may also channel women and minorities into certain jobs, which organizations feel are more suitable for them; for example, having a marketing role for a minority person so that they are better able to communicate with the ethnic minority consumers.

The skills of the underrepresented candidates are undervalued but as the researchers stated there is no reason why this should not go on in executive firms because that is exactly what goes on in organizations.[13]

By the same token there should be no reason why executive search firm consultants don't have the same biases that everyone else does. In one study, looking at both implicit and explicit attitudes towards women, it was found that the female consultants had a pro-female bias, whereas men had a pro-male bias. (It should be pointed out that this isn't typical, usually for senior level jobs women have a bias towards men the same way that men do.) The number of male consultants was considerably higher, however, than female consultants which meant that the male bias was greater overall. Having biases like this, however, whether it's pro-male or pro-female, doesn't give confidence in the fairness of the decisions that are being made.[14]

Other research has found that the executive search firms only seriously consider diversity when the client makes a firm request for it. Even then they will only focus on the aspects of the diversity that the client is interested in. As a consequence, gender diversity gets a greater look-in when it comes to executive search firms than any other characteristic.[15] Rather worryingly, when asked whether ethnicity was of concern to them these search firm representatives would say that often it was of no concern to the client; but they were also found to denigrate the skills of the minorities themselves, underestimating what they were capable of. Furthermore they would suggest that the minorities could do more to help themselves by presenting themselves better, developing further skills, etc.

The networks that the firms have do not sufficiently extend to those groups who are underrepresented in leadership positions or those positions that feed into leadership. There is also a reliance on minorities themselves to recommend people who they should be contacting. This is not unusual in the executive search world, but it's a continuation of the practice of placing much of the burden of achieving racial equality on the minorities themselves.[16]

It also highlights the lack of diversity that exists within executive search firms. If the diversity was there to begin with then the need to reach out to underrepresented managers and executives to find out from them who should be part of their networks wouldn't be necessary. The need for diversity is a question that such firms are increasingly being asked about, and it's something that they are keen to provide an answer for. Their websites offer advice and guidance on how to tackle bias for example, but there is very little about how they seek to eliminate biases in their own processes and people.

In examining the trends for talent acquisition in 2024, several of the large global executive search firms state that one of their developments is to hire on skills not on the prestige and status of previous employers. It's as clear an admission of failings when it comes to diversity and inclusion as you could possibly get.

Only now, in 2024 when I am writing this, is it recognized that the skills should be the focus of what is being sought. My response to this, for now, is I'll believe it when I see it. There are too many ingrained practices in the sector for them to be abandoned now for the sake of DEI.

Executive search firms have profited enormously from the WFT. They have positioned themselves as key to enable organizations to succeed with their talent management strategies. They all have their data sets which enable them to carry out benchmarking, and they have their profiles to help organizations determine the skills they should be seeking. All of this is useful, but fails to address the key issue of how they go about eliminating bias in the work that they do and in the people who are doing it. My experience of working with executive search firms on this has not been particularly enlightening.

They have a particular resentment to a question being asked about the possibility that they may not be entirely objective in the way that they carry out their work. And yet you would have thought this is something that they would welcome in order to demonstrate to the world that they take the topic of diversity, inclusion and bias as seriously for themselves as they suggest it should be for their clients. Research has shown time and time again that if you don't fit the profile of the leadership prototype, greater question marks hang over you. Assessments about people start as soon as they share their name or other facts about themselves. The classic research paradigm demonstrating this is one that we are all familiar with. Organizations are sent two CVs which are identical in all respects except for one. It may be that the name has changed or a detail altered such as showing support for an LGBTQ+ organization or indicating a disability. All other details remain exactly the same – the information that reveals educational qualifications, experience and skills is not altered. Yet that one change is enough to reduce the chances of being selected as a woman,[17] minority,[18] LGBTQ+ person[19] or a disabled person.[20] Given such stark findings as these, based on a simple adjustment of the details, why should we assume that somehow humanity has found a group of people, executive search firm consultants, who are somehow immune to such biases?

However, their activities have been under-researched and when it comes to bias, there are real concerns about the way they go about their business. When it comes to talent management and diversity, therefore, the role of the executive search firms needs to be explored a lot more closely, and greater scrutiny given to the processes they use and the way they go about making their decisions.

In the box there are some starter questions that can be posed to executive search firms to test their approach to seeking candidates, and also how they tackle issues of bias and fairness within their own firms.

When evaluating executive search firms for their ability to find suitably qualified diverse candidates, it's essential to ask targeted questions to assess their approach to diversity, equity and inclusion. Here are some questions to consider:

1 Track record and experience:

- What is your specific areas of expertise and specialism when it comes to finding diverse candidates?

- What percentage of your placements in the last 12 months have been female/minority/LGBTQ+/disabled candidates?

- Can you provide examples of successfully placing diverse candidates in roles similar to what we're looking for?

- How many of your team members specialize in diversity recruitment? What do they specialize in?

- What training have they had?

2 Diversity and inclusion approach:

- How do you ensure that you are attracting a diverse pool of candidates?

- What strategies do you use to identify and engage with female and minority candidates who may not be actively looking for new opportunities?

- How do you mitigate unconscious bias in the sourcing and screening process?

3 Networks and sourcing:

- What networks, affiliations or partnerships do you have that focus on diverse talent pipelines (e.g. women's leadership organizations, minority professional associations)?

- How do you source candidates from underrepresented groups, particularly in industries where diversity is less common?

- What outreach do you engage in to build relationships with diverse candidates over time?

4 Search process:

- How do you define and measure success when it comes to diverse placements?

- What steps do you take to ensure diverse candidates progress through the later stages of the recruitment process?
- How do you assess candidates' cultural alignment with our organization's diversity and inclusion goals?

5 Client and candidate advocacy:

- How do you advocate for diverse candidates when presenting them to clients?
- How do you handle situations where clients are resistant to considering diverse candidates?
- Can you provide client references who can speak to your success in recruiting diverse candidates?

6 Metrics and reporting:

- Do you track diversity metrics for your candidate pools, and will you share those with us throughout the search process?
- What percentage of your shortlists typically include diverse candidates?
- How do you report on the diversity of the candidate pool and placement outcomes during the search?

7 Retention and long-term success:

- How do you support retention and long-term success of diverse candidates after placement?
- Have you had repeat engagements with clients to continue improving diversity in their leadership teams?

8 Internal diversity commitment:

- What is the diversity make-up of your own leadership team and recruitment consultants?
- What internal diversity and inclusion policies and practices does your firm have in place?
- How inclusive is your own organization and what data do you have?

Key points

Over half a century ago Thomas Schelling demonstrated how small biases enacted over a long period of time had significant consequences in terms of community segregation. Once that occurs the possibility of tensions between different groups becomes more of a possibility. Recent research has demonstrated, by use of powerful statistical computing models, that the same conclusion can be reached about an organization and the decisions it makes about people, particularly when hiring. Small biases have significant consequences both in terms of selection and retention of underrepresented groups. It's essential therefore that organizations continue to review their attraction and selection processes to ensure that the systems are as fair as they can be. More critically, they need to ensure that individuals involved in making these significant decisions are trained in the tasks that have been delegated to them. A refusal to accept that bias may even be a possibility will ensure the perpetuation of unfairness to the detriment of diverse candidates, but also to the organization itself.

It has long been accepted by psychologists that whilst our personalities may mature, we have the same traits in adulthood that we displayed as children. Consequently, the game has been that we should be finding roles for ourselves that fit both with our interests and our personality traits. However, societal values and attitudes impact on our choices so that we can find ourselves failing to look at careers that might suit our dispositions but that go against expectations, particularly those based on gender. The longitudinal study of children in Hawaii shows how this is indeed the case. It also reveals how our personalities change in response to the jobs that we find ourselves in. Habitually working in a particular way, because our work demands it, has an impact in terms of the development of our personality traits.

In other words, the preoccupation that some talent theorists have about the fixed nature of our abilities is contradicted by such studies. A developmental approach to leadership is something that will benefit everyone, which will also enable greater diversity to be achieved in leadership roles – something that has continued to elude us.

McKinsey's widely accepted, but essentially flawed, War for Talent has benefited executive search firms considerably. They are now seen as a vital part of the machinery of talent management, yet their practices have not come under the scrutiny that their influence deserves. From the research that is available, there are biases evident in both the processes they operate and the individuals who operate them, which impacts the decisions made. From defining what a leader is through to searching for them and then selecting them, the limited evidence that exists suggests that they are as biased as anyone else. Why shouldn't they be – they are human after all.

Looking at executive search firms' websites it's clear they expend a lot of energy to ensure they project the right image when it comes to diversity and inclusion. Much of the talk, however, reveals their biased practices. They also say little about what they are doing in terms of their own firms, and how they seek to ensure that the processes and the people operating them are doing so fairly.

Notes

1 Office for National Statistics. Ethnic group – Census Maps, 2021, www.ons. gov.uk/census/maps/choropleth/identity/ethnic-group/ethnic-group-tb-6a/ asian-asian-british-or-asian-welsh (archived at https://perma.cc/9YWJ-GFYU)

2 T C Schelling. Models of segregation, *The American Economic Review*, 1969, 59 (2), 488–93

3 J H Hardy III, K S Tey, W Cyrus-Lai, R F Martell, A Olstad and E L Uhlmann. Bias in context: small biases in hiring evaluations have big consequences, *Journal of Management*, 2022, 48 (3), 657–92

4 L S Gottfriedson. Circumscription and compromise: a developmental theory of occupational aspirations, *Journal of Counselling Psychology*, 1981, 28 (6), 859–84

5 S A Woods and S E Hampson. Predicting adult occupational environments from gender and childhood personality traits, *Journal of Applied Psychology*, 2010, 95 (6), 1045

6 S A Woods, G W Edmonds, S E Hampson and F Lievens. How our work influences who we are: testing a theory of vocational and personality development over fifty years, *Journal of Research in Personality*, 2020, 85, 103930

7 A Tilcsik, M Anteby and C R Knight. Concealable stigma and occupational segregation: toward a theory of gay and lesbian occupations, *Administrative Science Quarterly*, 2015, 60 (3), 446–81

8 J R Faulconbridge, J V Beaverstock, S Hall and A Hewitson. The 'war for talent': the gatekeeper role of executive search firms in elite labour markets, *Geoforum*, 2009, 40 (5), 800–08

9 AESC. The History of Executive Search, no date, www.aesc.org/insights/blog/history-executive-search (archived at https://perma.cc/MQ2G-FDWG)

10 P Cappelli and M Hamori. Understanding executive job search, *Organization Science*, 2014, 25 (5), 1511–29

11 J R Faulconbridge, J V Beaverstock, S Hall and A Hewitson. The 'war for talent': the gatekeeper role of executive search firms in elite labour markets, *Geoforum*, 2009, 40 (5), 800–08

12 G F Dreher, J Y Lee and T A Clerkin. Mobility and cash compensation: the moderating effects of gender, race, and executive search firms, *Journal of Management*, 2011, 37 (3), 651–81

13 Ibid.

14 R Siegel, C J König and Y Zobel. Executive search consultants' biases against women (or men?), *Frontiers in Psychology*, 2020, 11, 541766

15 C Holgersson, J Tienari, S Meriläinen and R Bendl. Executive search as ethnosociality: a cross-cultural comparison, *International Journal of Cross Cultural Management*, 2016, 16 (2), 153–69

16 M Trudgett, S Page and S K Coates. Talent war: recruiting Indigenous senior executives in Australian universities, *Journal of Higher Education Policy and Management*, 2021, 43 (1), 110–24

17 A A Eaton, J F Saunders, R K Jacobson and K West. How gender and race stereotypes impact the advancement of scholars in STEM: professors' biased evaluations of physics and biology post-doctoral candidates, *Sex Roles*, 2020, 82, 127–41

18 OECD (2013) Discrimination against immigrants – measurement, incidence and policy instruments, in *International Migration Outlook 2013*, OECD Publishing, Paris, https://doi.org/10.1787/migr_outlook-2013-7-en (archived at https://perma.cc/PYY9-XF4B)

19 K B Bryant-Lees and M E Kite. Evaluations of LGBT job applicants: consequences of applying 'out', *Equality, Diversity and Inclusion: An International Journal*, 2021, 40 (7), 874–91

20 M Ameri, L Schur, M Adya, F S Bentley, P McKay and D Kruse. The disability employment puzzle: a field experiment on employer hiring behavior, *ILR Review*, 2018, 71 (2), 329–64

5

Performance management and bias

Overview

At the beginning of the 19th century, each of the workers at the New Lanark mills in Scotland was presented with a new gadget suspended above their workstation. It was a rectangular block of wood painted a different colour on four of its sides: white, yellow, blue and black. As a piece of equipment, it was very simple, but it was the way that it was used that was remarkable.

Each day one of the sides would be visible, and that would represent an assessment of the worker's behaviour on the previous day. White was for 'super excellence', yellow for 'moderate goodness', blue for 'a neutral state of morals' and black was for 'excessive naughtiness'.[1] Known as the Silent Monitor it was a precursor of the modern-day performance management system. Developed by the mill owner Robert Owen, the categories reflect the times. The last category 'excessive naughtiness' reads like something a primary school teacher would reprimand one of their young children for. In fact, that was the case because many of the workers in the factories were children. The owner of the mill, Robert Owen, was determined to improve the conditions under which his workers laboured. In his time, he cut the hours that were worked during the day so that children were able to receive some education.

The Silent Monitor measured a person's conduct on the previous day and made the assessment public. In addition, Owen also measured inputs, outputs and wages earned for everyone. It was, in other words, a system that wasn't just concerned about productivity, but the way in which people carried out their work. Today we would refer to this as a measure of values rather than an assessment of their morality, but it amounts to much the same thing. It was concerned with what you did and how you did it.

Performance management has developed and evolved since then. As management came to be seen as worthy of study in and of itself and was seen as a profession, so performance management came to assume greater importance. Writing in 1920, W D Scott recognized some of the significant changes that were taking place in the management of people.[2] It was important, Scott stated, that people continued to learn and be developed. He identified a number of ways in which management of personnel could be improved and the first of these was in the recognition of 'equality of man'. Philosophers, he acknowledged, had considered this topic for centuries, and his fundamental point was that we needed to ensure that we were treating people fairly in our organizations. He also acknowledged that decisions that we make at work are not always rational and that emotional reactions lead to a lack of equality and fairness.

The 1950s onwards saw the development of an HR profession, which had the dual focus of control and welfare.[3] The 1970s saw a growing concern about discriminatory practices in organizations, and, with it, more attention being paid to the fairness of the systems that were operating in organizations, with increased attention given to the ways in which performance was measured, which led to the increased use of rating scales.[4]

Since then, performance management systems have been recognized as a key process for employee engagement and motivation. There's also been increased use of 360-degree feedback to gain greater insight into how individuals are seen by others, including their line manager, colleagues and direct reports. Technology today also enables us to gather data on individuals much more quickly.

Performance management, of course, is more than just an annual review meeting. It's an elaborate and complex process which requires a whole host of skills for it to be enacted properly.

There are several elements to performance management which start with an articulation of the organizational aims and its values. This then translates into the goals and objectives for every individual in the organization. There should then be ongoing discussion and reviews with individuals as the year progresses. Discussions will take place about individual's development needs and a plan to address them, which will also be reviewed during the year. This culminates in an annual performance review, which will be linked directly or indirectly to the person's remuneration and recognition. As if this wasn't enough, the performance management system is also the basis of identifying people with the potential to move into more senior roles. It's a critical process in organizations doing a lot of the heavy lifting in making judgements about people's performance, potential and progression

There are essentially two elements to the process: evaluation and development.

By their very nature, they are in tension with one another. The former requires line managers to be focused on the data, entirely objective in providing an assessment of performance, which should be done rationally, fairly and with precision. The latter requires emphasis to be on the person themselves, rather than data. The line manager will be required to be empathetic, and to have an acceptance that everyone needs opportunities to learn and develop.

Bias in appraisal process

Imagine working in an office where an experienced and senior individual asks a colleague to create an Excel spreadsheet to evaluate women on their 'tit size, ass shape and leg length', and where sexism like this was seemingly routine and accepted.

Imagine working in an environment where speaking out against behaviour like this would lead to the complainant being punished. Would it be a surprise to learn that in such an organization very few women would be:

- able to give of their best?

- identified as future leaders?
- in senior positions?

Jamie Fiore Higgins worked in such an organization, which she describes in her book *Bully Market: My story of money and misogyny at Goldman Sachs.*[5] The book contains numerous examples of sexist and misogynistic behaviour, but it didn't end there. She recounts the discriminatory ways in which minorities and the LGBTQ+ community were treated as well. It's not hard to understand that we cannot divorce performance from the climate in which it is being carried out. Working in an organization that displays such prejudice against a variety of groups will have a detrimental impact on individuals' self-esteem, sense of safety and, ultimately, performance.

Higgins' book has many blatant examples of sexist, racist and homophobic behaviour. In many organizations, however, there are subtle of ways of being prejudiced. Analysis of performance management reports highlights the ways in which the stereotypes of out groups, described in Chapter 2, impact the way in which their performance is measured and their potential assessed.

Much of the work, it must be said, has examined gender with very consistent results. More recently, attention has been paid to other out groups.

Performance management and gender

The stereotypes of women are that they are communal; that is, warm and interested in relationships. Furthermore, they are not considered as agentic as men; that is, they are seen as less assertive and less likely to be directing and influencing a group. Women who conform to the stereotypes are liked more, but those who act in a counter-stereotypical way are less accepted and judged more harshly. Agentic behaviours, however, are precisely the ones that are more likely to see somebody promoted. Which then leaves women in a double bind: behave in a stereotypically feminine way and be liked but not be seen as having potential to progress. Or behave in a counter-stereotypical way, displaying requisite leadership potential, but receive harsher judgements from people.

The conundrum that women face was captured in a very helpful way by researchers Ginka Toegel and Jean-Louis Barsoux at IMD Business School in Switzerland. Table 5.1 lists behaviours associated with agency and communality.

Toegel and Barsoux found, as many others have, that whereas men could display a range of agentic behaviours, women, if they wished to progress, had to avoid being on the extreme of either end because this had negative consequences in terms of how they were perceived and their performance judged.

It's worth looking at this list in detail. We can see how the behaviours on the right of the table are not those we see many women performing in the workplace. A woman leading in this dominant way, which is a mixture of assertion, confidence, impatience and aggression, would soon find out how poorly appreciated her behaviour is. On the other hand, it is not only more acceptable for a man to be behaving in this way, but they are more likely to be admired for it.

TABLE 5.1 Avoiding the extremes: leadership behaviour assessed by agency and communality

Highly communal	Moderately communal	Neutral	Moderately agentic	Highly agentic
Putting welfare of others above own	Smiling	Participating in work discussions	Gesticulating	Pointing
Speaking softly	Nodding	Providing, seeking or summarizing information	Sitting at the head of the table	Table tapping
Enquiring about family	Open-handed gestures		Standing when others sit	Staring
Gossiping	Giving recognition to others	Composed demeanour	Holding someone's gaze	Husky voice
Giggling	Sharing credit	Self-deprecating humour	Low pitched voice	Talking sports
	Active listening	Level voice	Shrugging	Sarcasm
	Responsiveness	Listening calmly	Shaking head	Yelling/raising voice
	Thanking people publicly		Sighing	Public put-down
	Speaking out against injustice		Slow vocal cadence	Swearing
	Asking for or offering help		Speaking up first	
	Showing concern			

Women leaders and managers behaving in more stereotypically male ways will be assessed more negatively as it is a violation of social norms and expectations.[6] This is a manifestation of what was discussed in Chapter 2, of the considerable overlap between the stereotype of a man and the stereotype of a leader.[7]

The performance management consultancy organization Textio has a long history of looking at the language used in performance reviews and the type of feedback people are given. Dr Kieran Snyder, Textio's CEO, examined in detail 248 performance reviews from 180 people (105 men, 75 women).[8] Her key findings were:

1 Women were more likely to receive critical feedback. 71 per cent of the 248 performance reviews examined contained critical feedback. However, gender differences were apparent with women receiving critical feedback on 87.9 per cent of occasions compared with 58.9 per cent of occasions for men.

2 Men and women received different types of feedback. Both groups received constructive suggestions in terms of how they can improve their performance, but it was noticeably different for men and women. Men's feedback was focused on how they can develop their skills further. For example, 'there were a few cases where it would've been extremely helpful if you had gone deeper into the details to help moving area forward'. Women would receive this type of constructive feedback also, but another element to the feedback was that they should, in Snyder's words, 'pipe down'. For example, 'You can come across as abrasive sometimes. I know you don't mean to, but you need to pay attention to your tone.' This is described as negative personality criticism and the differences between men and women were stark: in the 83 critical reviews for men, feedback of this type was given on only two occasions, and in the 94 critical reviews for women, it was 71 occasions.

3 The manager's gender isn't a factor. There are no differences between male and female managers in terms of the observations made and the feedback given. This is, in fact, consistent with other research, which shows that, when it comes to stereotypes, including those related to leadership, women have the same biases as men.

Women were far more likely to receive feedback about their personality than men were. Adjectives such as bossy, abrasive, strident, emotional and irrational were used only for women. Aggressive was used for both women and men, but very differently. Women were criticized for showing too much of this characteristic, whereas on two out of the three occasions it was used as feedback to men, it was that they needed to be more aggressive.

When analysed by the high-performing employees, only 2 per cent of the men received negative feedback. The corresponding number for the high-performing women was a staggering 76 per cent.

This research has been backed up with a more recent and larger piece of research, looking at people's experiences of performance feedback, as well as an analysis of written appraisals of people's work. The data was analysed looking at a wide range of demographic variables.[9] The resulting analysis was illuminating as well as comprehensive.

88 per cent of people had received feedback relating to personality traits. Such feedback is harder to turn into a developmental action plan because it's addressing things that are seen as core to who you are. Behavioural feedback, on the other hand, is something that you can work to change. Three-quarters of the men had received personality-related feedback compared to 100 per cent of women, non-binary and gender fluid individuals. Participants were also asked to state which adjectives had been used to describe them (see Figure 5.1). Women were more than twice as likely to be described as 'collaborative' and 'nice'. They were over 50 per cent more likely to be described as 'helpful'. Given these very positive relationship-oriented adjectives it's surprising then to find that they are seven times more likely to be described as 'opinionated' and 11 times more likely to be seen as 'abrasive'.

Men were three times more likely to be described as 'confident' and nearly four times more likely to be described as 'ambitious'.

Women are appreciated if they stayed in their lane, which is to be supportive, helpful and contribute to the positive vibes within a team. Move away from that, by being more critical or expressing an opinion,

FIGURE 5.1 Personality feedback received, by gender

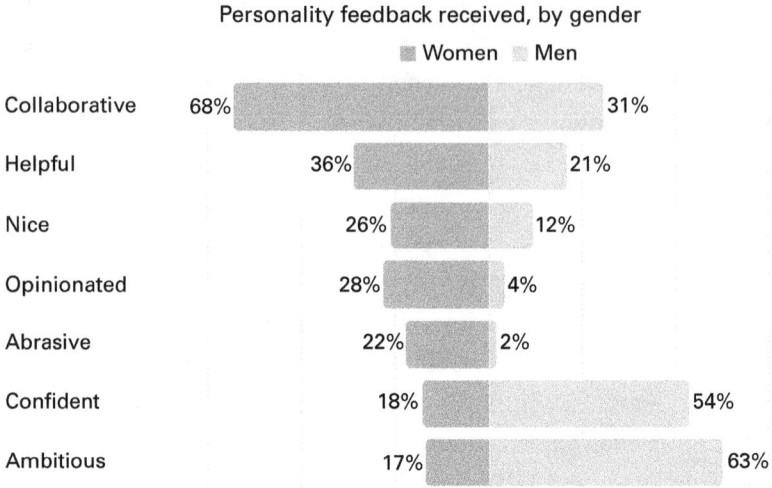

Personality feedback received, by gender

Women   Men

	Women	Men
Collaborative	68%	31%
Helpful	36%	21%
Nice	26%	12%
Opinionated	28%	4%
Abrasive	22%	2%
Confident	18%	54%
Ambitious	17%	63%

Survey question: "Which of these traits have you most often heard people use to describe you at work?"

and they aren't appreciated so much. Men are given feedback to improve on some of their behaviours, but women's faults are seen as being more about their character, which will be more difficult to change.

Written performance feedback for 25,000 people was also examined, and it was found that women were twice as likely to receive feedback that wasn't actionable compared to men. The research team also looked at exaggerated feedback, where words such as 'never', 'always' and 'constantly' are used. Examples the authors give include 'you never show up on time', 'you always bring a curious mindset to every conversation', 'you are constantly looking for ways to improve things'. Women received more exaggerated feedback than men, which sounds like a good thing, right? Such feedback, however, is inaccurate, untrue and unhelpful. The problem with such feedback is that there's not a lot you can do with it, even when it's intended to be complimentary. Exaggerated feedback is more likely therefore to be discounted or not believed.

The extent to which a behaviour is seen in the workplace is one way of evaluating gender differences in performance management. What we are not able to determine is whether this was a bias on the part of the manager or whether it was an accurate description. This was what Shelley Correll and her colleagues set out to discover.[10] They didn't just look at what line managers saw in people's behaviour but how they valued it. Consistent with other research, women were rated more highly on being helpful, whereas men were rated higher on characteristics related to taking charge. This is important, not just because it demonstrates again that women are viewed less favourably when taking charge, but because they also found that this behaviour had a strong relationship with the overall performance rating that someone received. In other words, this one factor, taking charge, was weighted more highly by line managers than other factors, including being helpful. They also found that when women displayed leadership behaviours, they were valued less highly than when men displayed them.

There were no differences between men and women on the number of references made to someone's potential. Men and women had very similar types of comments about the development they needed to improve their performance. Despite all of this, women were rated as having less potential than men, which reveals some residual doubts about whether they could perform in more senior and challenging roles in the future. This highlights another issue when it comes to underrepresented groups at senior levels and organizations – they experience what is referred to as the 'higher scrutiny bar'. It is in effect a set of double standards, where underrepresented groups, in this case women, must achieve a higher level of performance to be considered as having the potential to progress.

Gender differences were also found in something known as exceptionalism – those individuals who are outstanding in their work – precisely those people who the WFT is targeted at. It was a clear area of difference between the two sexes, with men being seen as exceptional more often and being valued more highly because of it.

Performance management and race

In research we have carried out at Pearn Kandola, racial minorities in organizations experience much more discrimination and exclusion than their white peers. 60 per cent of black people and 42 per cent of

Asian people have said they experienced racial discrimination in the workplace. Of those, approximately 12 per cent had experienced the most direct, hostile and blatant forms of racism in being physically and verbally abused. Most people had experienced more subtle forms, however, which is referred to as modern racism, the biggest form of which is making assumptions about someone's ability and character. This was reported by 39 per cent of black participants and 53 per cent of Asians. Furthermore, 45 per cent of black respondents and 31 per cent of Asians said they had been treated differently at work. 28 per cent of black people and 23 per cent of Asians said they had been actively excluded from events and activities in the workplace. Being helped and feeling supported in the workplace has an impact not just on individual performance but on organizational outcomes too.[11] As was mentioned in Chapter 2, acts of discrimination and of exclusion have an impact on people's wellbeing as well as them not feeling respected or valued.

When people start to feel excluded, the lack of safety they experience will mean that they will withdraw from others in the workplace. This could then lead to a downward spiral where the lack of engagement from the individual will lead to others on their team excluding them more. Good relationships are essential for someone to have a sense of acceptance in the workplace, which means also recognizing that sometimes people won't necessarily be in the best of moods and not punishing them for it.[12] In situations where people don't feel included they are more likely to also view themselves negatively, they are more likely to disregard positive feedback or compliments that they receive (for example by ascribing a great outcome to luck), and they will feel less confident.[13] Overall this will have a negative impact on their performance, something that will be readily seen by those around them. What won't be reflected upon though is that this may be due to the discrimination and exclusion that they are experiencing.

In reviewing the literature regarding race and performance management in my book *Racism at Work*[14] I summarized some of the key issues:

- appraisal ratings and anti-minority bias
- appraisal ratings and pro-majority bias

- assessment of capabilities and development
- attributing success

Appraisal ratings and anti-minority bias. In comparison to gender, fewer studies have been carried out looking at appraisal ratings given to different racial groups. The appointment of new judges in the USA, however, is a public process and so it was possible for researchers to analyse the fairness and objectivity of the process. The American Bar Association assesses each of the shortlisted candidates on three criteria: integrity, professional competence and judicial temperament. An analysis of the decisions made showed that, even when the candidates had equivalent qualifications and experience, women and minorities were more likely to receive a rating of 'not adequate' than white male candidates, so revealing an anti-minority bias as well as an anti-female one.[15]

Appraisal ratings and pro-majority bias. Often when people talk about discrimination in the workplace it's assumed that it will be a bias against a particular group of people. It's something that we need to be careful about; however, it may not always be that a minority group has been poorly or harshly treated, but rather that the majority group has been treated leniently. For example, a group of partners in a law firm were given a report to examine. All the partners received the same reports but the name of the person was changed suggesting that it had either been written by a white lawyer or an ethnic minority one. There were mistakes in the report and more of them were picked up when the author was a minority that if they were white. These were mistakes and the minorities, quite rightly, were being picked up on them. The bias, however, was evident in terms of showing leniency towards a white lawyer, making them look better than they were. Ironically, such leniency would have done no favours for the firm had these reports been sent out to a client.[16] The research revealed that law firm partners had an expectation that minorities would make more mistakes possibly due to a belief that their English was not as good as their white peers. This made them extra vigilant when looking at reports written by minorities.

The degree of scrutiny given to the minorities in fact was something that should've been applied to all the reports, which would then have meant better quality all round.

Assessment of capabilities and development. Research has consistently shown that minorities in the workplace receive less constructive feedback which has a negative impact on the development of the skills and their progression.[17] Snyder's research examining the language used in performance management looked at race as well as gender. In overall terms, black and Latinx received the least amount of feedback compared to other minority groups. Black men fared the worst, receiving only 68 per cent of the written feedback that was given to white women. As we have noted earlier, feedback relating to personality is the least actionable, as it deals with something core to the individual, as opposed to feedback given in behavioural terms.

For every piece of feedback that was not actionable given to white men under 40, white women over the age of 40 received 4.4 times more such comments, and black women received 8.8 times more.

Black and Latinx were also the ethnic groups that were most likely to receive exaggerated feedback – the sort that is hyped up, less credible and more likely to be discounted.

It all points to a picture where minority groups are having to prove themselves all the time, and are confronted by managers who are more likely to scrutinize their work as well as having low expectations of them. As a demonstration of the last point, Snyder found that minorities were more likely to be described as 'overachieving' which she states is 'typically applied to strong performers transcending low expectations—is much more frequently applied to women and people of colour. In the eyes of the feedback provider, brilliant geniuses are expected to perform well; overachievers perform well despite having inherent limitations.' This shows how managers are applying a fixed mindset approach to people, believing that some groups have natural talents, and others having to work hard to overcome their limitations. This has implications because it will mean that overachievers will be less likely to be given assignments that stretch and develop them further because they have already gone beyond their natural capabilities.

Attributing success. Attributing success is also subject to re-interpretation based on the stereotypes that we hold about different groups of people. Where minorities have been successful as leaders, their achievements are more likely to be attributed to external factors rather than their inherent leadership qualities.[18,19]

In her book *The Social Psychology of Organizations*, psychologist Joanna Wilde reviewed performance management systems in an organization. Race had an impact on performance appraisals in very subtle but significant ways. As with the research on gender, minorities were being judged by different standards. White staff were the benchmark because they were evaluated against something referred to as 'high standards'.

Asian staff, by her review of the comments that were made about them, were implicitly being assessed on qualities of diligence and accuracy. Black staff, on the other hand, were mostly being judged against criteria related to leadership, being a team player and time-keeping. When a black person was late for work or an appointment, this would have an impact on their performance ratings, whereas lateness was something that had no significance for white staff at all. She also reported that when a black leader succeeded it was attributed to factors not associated with leadership, a good team for example, but when they failed it was seen as an indication that they did not have the qualities needed to be a leader. All of which shows that there are many biases which impact the way people are viewed, assessed and managed in the workplace. Without acknowledging this we cannot ensure that we are identifying, developing and managing talent in any way that could be considered valid.

Key points

In much of the talent management literature there is the persistent belief that highly talented individuals will reveal themselves in the workplace. Having been identified, they should be coveted and developed for the benefit of themselves and for the organizations they work in.

This totally ignores the fact that managers are not objective in the assessments they make about the people who work for them. It also overlooks the way stereotypes associated with underrepresented groups have an effect on the ways in which they are perceived and, consequently, the judgements that are made about them.

Stereotyping is one of the reasons why there are so few women in senior leadership roles. In overall terms, women are stereotypically viewed as being communal with a greater interest in relationships and displaying qualities such as being caring, compassionate and empathetic.

Men are stereotypically viewed as being agentic-directing, driving performance and getting things done–qualities which overlap considerably with those required of a leader. In any talent management process therefore men are favoured from the beginning. Women are perfectly capable of demonstrating leadership qualities; the problem being that when they do so they suffer penalties such as being liked less and viewed as abrasive. This conundrum that women face is referred to as a double bind: act in the expected way and you won't be seen as a leader, but displaying leadership qualities is counter-stereotypical and will not be appreciated either.

Being viewed in stereotypical ways is one of the most common forms of discrimination that minorities experience in the workplace.

Feelings of exclusion and the experience of discrimination affects people's wellbeing and ultimately their performance. Where individuals are not supported by their colleagues and don't feel safe, they are more likely to withdraw from them thus making the situation worse. What is seen by their colleagues and line manager is somebody who is not performing, but what is not known about them is the reasons why this is happening.

Being able to speak up about one's experiences of not being valued and respected is very difficult. A psychologist recently asked for some advice on how to deal with minorities in the health profession. When discussing conduct issues and complaints with them, she said that they would accept the mistake that had been made and would also refer to the discrimination that they had experienced.

My initial thought was that she wanted advice on how to handle these conversations, instead she wanted to know how to respond when, to use her words, 'they played the race card'. She was, as a white psychologist, prepared to discuss the mistakes that had been made and to recommend the appropriate disciplinary measures, but she was totally unwilling to listen to any mitigating circumstances that might have impacted their performance. This lack of reflection and understanding of the experiences of minorities and others in the workplace means that we will continue to view under-performance as something related solely to the individual.

We will fail to acknowledge the stress that is caused by being excluded and furthermore we will accept that the people who are performing well do so based entirely on their own capabilities.

Performance management is an extremely complicated process. It puts demands on line managers in a way that nothing else does and requires them to have a whole variety of skills to be able to practice it well. Organizations tend to place the greatest emphasis on the actual procedures, with extensive information and guidance typically being provided. However, what is really needed is training so that people understand the component parts that make up a performance management system and are able to develop and practice the skills that are required.

In addition, organizations should carry out regular reviews of their processes, garnering feedback in a confidential way from different groups of people in the organization to understand their experiences of the process. The one-off staff survey undertaken annually will provide some information but the central importance of performance management requires us to do something that examines this in more detail on a regular basis.

Individuals don't have to be passive in response to the feedback that they receive. Minorities and women are more likely to be given personality-related feedback, the type that is least actionable.

In those situations, Snyder recommends people ask:

- 'Can you give me a couple of recent examples?'
- 'Can you describe another way I could approach that?'
- 'What specific changes would you recommend that I make?'

There is so much that hinges on the performance management process that it is entirely negligent not to examine in detail the way that it is being used and the biases, often very subtle, that impede us in making objective and fair decisions about people.

Performance management systems determine who will be identified as the future talent, but as we have seen the way in which this determination is made is affected by the stereotypes that we hold, the discrimination and exclusion that people experience, and the way we choose to attribute success.

Notes

1 R Donkin (2001) *Blood, Sweat and Tears: The evolution of work*, Texere Publishing

2 W D Scott. Changes in some of our conceptions and practices of personnel, *Psychological Review*, 1920, 27 (2), 81–94

3 K J Rotich. History, evolution and development of human resource management: a contemporary perspective, *Global Journal of Human Resource Management*, 2015, 3 (3), 58–73

4 A S DeNisi and K R Murphy. Performance appraisal and performance management: 100 years of progress? *Journal of Applied Psychology*, 2017, 102 (3), 421

5 J F Higgins (2022) *Bully Market: My story of money and misogyny at Goldman Sachs*, Simon and Schuster

6 A H Eagly, M G Makhijani and B G Klonsky. Gender and the evaluation of leaders: a meta-analysis, *Psychological Bulletin*, 1992, 111 (1), 3

7 A M Koenig, A H Eagly, A A Mitchell and T Ristikari. Are leader stereotypes masculine? A meta-analysis of three research paradigms, *Psychological Bulletin*, 2011, 137 (4), 616

8 K Snyder. The abrasiveness trap: high-achieving men and women are described differently in reviews, *Fortune Magazine*, 2014, 26, 8–14

9 Textio. Language Bias in Performance Feedback, 2022, https://explore.textio.com/feedback-bias/language-bias-in-performance-feedback?utm_campaign=textio_social&utm_source=linkedin&utm_medium=social#page=1&zoom=100 (archived at https://perma.cc/G6KB-LDZH)

10 S J Correll, K R Weisshaar, A T Wynn and J D Wehner. Inside the Black Box of organizational life: the gendered language of performance assessment *American Sociological Review*, 2020, 85 (6), 1022–50, https://doi.org/10.1177/0003122420962080 (archived at https://perma.cc/Z5AA-RFQJ)

11 P M Podsakoff and S B MacKenzie. Impact of organizational citizenship behavior on organizational performance: a review and suggestions for future research, *Organizational Citizenship Behavior and Contextual Performance*, 2014, 133–51

12 J P Forgas. Affective influences on self-disclosure: mood effects on the intimacy and reciprocity of disclosing personal information, *Journal of Personality and Social Psychology*, 2011, 100 (3), 449

13 J P Forgas (2006) Affective influences on interpersonal behavior: toward understanding the role of affect in everyday interactions, in J P Forgas (ed), *Affect in Social Thinking and Behavior*, Psychology Press, New York, 269–89

14 R S Kandola (2018) *Racism at Work: The danger of indifference*, Pearn Kandola Publishing, Oxford

15 M Sen. How judicial qualification ratings may disadvantage minority and female candidates, *Journal of Law and Courts*, 2014, 2 (1), 33–65

16 A N Reeves (2014) *Written in Black & White: Exploring confirmation bias in racialized perceptions of writing skill*, Nextion, Chicago

17 M Wyatt and J Silvester. Reflections on the labyrinth: investigating black and minority ethnic leaders' career experiences, *Human Relations*, 2015, 68 (8), 1243–69, https://doi.org/10.1177/0018726714550890 (archived at https://perma.cc/WK3L-YA5U)

18 A M Carton and A S Rosette. Explaining bias against black leaders: integrating theory on information processing and goal-based stereotyping, *Academy of Management Journal*, 2011, 54 (6), 1141–58

19 M Wyatt and J Silvester. Reflections on the labyrinth: investigating black and minority ethnic leaders' career experiences, *Human Relations*, 2015, 68 (8), 1243–69, https://doi.org/10.1177/0018726714550890 (archived at https://perma.cc/WK3L-YA5U)

6

Identifying and developing talent

Leadership prototypes: What do we expect from the leader?

> When I walked into the room I was asked if I'm the IT guy. People were surprised when I told them that I was leading this group. (Ethnic minority leader working in France who recounted this experience to me)

Many of us, research tells us, are likely to have mental images about what a leader looks like, how they behave and how they sound. In this case the person of colour was presumed to be a technician or a specialist of some sort, but certainly not the leader.

The way in which we categorize and recognize leaders is known as the Leadership Categorization Theory (LCT).[1] There are two related concepts at the core of LCT:

1 First, we hold preconceived ideas of what a leader looks like and what constitutes effective leadership.

2 Second, these ideas significantly influence how leaders are perceived, selected and evaluated.

Every day we are bombarded with information via all of our senses, and, in order to make sense of the world, we simplify by organizing information into categories. These categories, also referred to as mental models or schemas, guide how we process information and when applied to leadership, they influence how we identify, recognize and react to leaders in organizational and social contexts. And they are powerful, sometimes making us fail to see what's going on right in front of us. Take this example from a senior female leader I met, who had recently been promoted as head of a business division and had just moved to a new location. On her first morning, she was making her way to her office:

> I was in the lift and overheard two guys talking to each other about their new boss they were about to meet. One said 'I'm not sure how long she'll last. She well probably get pregnant and we won't see her again.' I thought to myself 'It's going to be interesting when I introduce myself to them.'

Even though the two men knew that the recently appointed head of the business was female, the schema of a leader as male was so powerful, it never occurred to them that the unknown woman standing in the lift with them could possibly have been their new boss.

When we look at another person to determine whether they are a leader, we compare that individual against our prototype of a leader. A person is more likely to be categorized as a leader if their appearance and behaviour matches the leadership prototype.

Leadership prototypes typically include traits such as decisiveness, confidence, intelligence and charisma as well as aggression, dominance and assertiveness.

Our perceptions of leaders have vertical and horizontal dimensions to them. On the vertical plane there are three levels: superordinate, basic and subordinate. At the highest level, superordinate, we make a distinction between leaders and non-leaders. At the next level, basic, we distinguish between different types of leaders, for example in business, military and politics. At the subordinate level, we make further distinctions, for example in business technology, retail and engineering. These distinctions are important because we see greater diversity in leadership in some areas rather than others, for example there are more female leaders in the voluntary sector than in the private sector. Leadership segregation serves a purpose because it shows that it's not that women or minorities can't be leaders, it's just that they are better suited to specific industries or organizations.

How categorization affects leadership perception

Leadership categorization theory highlights the importance of followers' perceptions in the leadership process. When followers observe someone in a position of authority or influence, they unconsciously evaluate that person against their internal leadership prototypes. If the individual looks and acts the way we expect a leader to behave, in line with these prototypes, the person is more likely to be viewed as a legitimate and effective leader. On the other hand, if the individual differs significantly from the prototype, they may struggle to be recognized as a leader, regardless of their actual competence or influence.

The prototype therefore moves us down a biased path from the very beginning. From then on the biases can start to accumulate. When a leader fits the prototype, followers are more likely to attribute positive qualities to them, often unrelated to their actual performance. Known as the 'halo effect', it is where the categorization itself enhances the perception of the leader's abilities, creating a self-fulfilling prophecy. Conversely, leaders who do not fit the prototype face greater scrutiny, scepticism or even rejection, a process referred to as the 'horns effect'.

The categorization process has several important implications for leadership and organizational dynamics because it will impact:

1 **Leader emergence:** Those people who we believe have the potential to be the leaders of the future

2 **Leader effectiveness:** Perceived alignment with leadership prototypes can also influence assessments of a leader's effectiveness. Even if two leaders perform the same tasks with similar outcomes, the one who more closely matches the group's prototype may be viewed as more competent and successful.

3 **Leader-follower dynamics:** Leadership is as much about the followers as it is about the leader. Followers' expectations and perceptions shape the leadership process, making leadership a relational and co-constructed phenomenon. The categorization process influences how followers respond to the leader. If the leader

fits the prototype, followers are more likely to support and follow their directives. If not, they may resist or undermine the leader's authority.

4 **Attributions and evaluations:** Once categorized, the leader's actions are interpreted through the lens of leadership. Positive outcomes are attributed to the leader's competence, while negative outcomes may be downplayed or attributed to external factors. Conversely, if the individual is not seen as a leader, even positive outcomes might not enhance their standing within the group.

5 **Cultural differences:** Leadership prototypes are not universally fixed and can vary across cultures and contexts. In collectivist cultures, for example, leadership prototypes may emphasize group harmony, consensus and modesty, whereas in individualistic cultures, leadership prototypes may prioritize autonomy, assertiveness and individual achievement. This cultural variability adds complexity to leadership categorization and underscores the importance of context in leadership studies.

Leadership and gender

Leadership prototypes aren't something that's discussed so openly in workplaces but every now and then these biases burst into the light. Take the now infamous email distributed to all staff by a software engineer at Google commenting on the drive for diversity and inclusion, giving reasons why there were fewer women in leadership roles:

> We always ask why we don't see women in top leadership positions, but we never ask why we see so many men in these jobs. These positions often require long, stressful hours that may not be worth it if you want a balanced and fulfilling life. Status is the primary metric that men are judged on, pushing many men into these higher paying, less satisfying jobs for the status that they entail.[2]

In addition to men having the motivation to seek out these roles, the email goes on to explain that there are also natural differences between the sexes in personality and abilities. It should only be expected therefore that men and women will gravitate towards different roles based on their interests and capabilities. This is a more popular view than we might think, essentially promoting the sentiment 'Men are from Mars, Women are from Venus',[3] popularized in the book of the same name by John Gray. (I prefer the philosophy of the great comedian George Carlin: 'Men are from earth and women are from earth. Get over it.')

Rigorous academic analyses have shown time and again that there is little or no difference in leadership capabilities and potential between men and women. In 1924 in the monumental work *An Introduction to the Science of Sociology*, it was remarked:

> Such a marked differentiation as there is between the adult man and the adult woman certainly does not exist in childhood. Similarly in respect of many other qualities, alike bodily and mental, in respect of many inclinations and numerous activities, we find that in childhood sexual differentiation is less marked than it is in adult life.[4]

A meta-analysis conducted in 1995 of over 80 studies on leadership found that women were as equally effective as leaders as men.[5] There was an indication in the study that men as followers were less likely to accept women as leaders, which reduced their effectiveness.

The authors of the influential *Organizational Behaviour*[6] provided their conclusion after having reviewed the research on six differences in leadership:

> the evidence suggests that the best place to begin is with the recognition that there are few, if any, important differences between men and women that will affect their job performance. There are, for instance, no consistent male–female differences in problem-solving ability, analytical skills, competitive drive, motivation, sociability or learning agility.

Finding that the main sex differences found in a meta-analysis was men's ability to throw objects further than women, the authors commented wryly:

> So unless leadership positions require the CEO to throw the quarterly report the length of the conference table, it would not appear that women have less potential than men to become managers and leaders.[7]

Is that enough? OK just one more then. This time British psychologists Steve Woods and Michael West found on reviewing the literature that there was little difference in the leadership styles and performance of men and women and that when differences were found they were 'so small in fact that it is safe to assume that there is no difference in leadership effectiveness between men and women'.[8]

The differences we see in the leadership styles of men and women exist because we want them to exist. Our beliefs about what a leader looks like, and the roles that men and women should be playing, influence our perceptions of what we see going on around us.

One of the world's leading psychometric organizations conducted a large-scale project comparing leadership profiles of men and women. Mining their data on cognitive ability tests and personality, they compared them to the specification of a leader. The dataset was huge: 1,118,197 profiles. One in 15 people overall had the potential to be a leader and there were no differences between men and women. Table 6.1 provides the results from 25 countries and shows the number of women who were in leadership roles in those countries at that time. Just as other authors and academics have found, despite the stereotypes, men were just as communal as women, and women were just as agentic as men.

Perceptions of a leader, lack of fit, lack of access to networks and lack of mentors and sponsors are all issues that are faced by other underrepresented groups in leadership, including ethnic minorities, sexual minorities and disabled people.

Disability

Employers make many assumptions about people with disabilities, including:

- lack of productivity
- poorer quality of work
- higher levels of absenteeism

TABLE 6.1 Gender and leadership

Leaders for today rank	Country	% of men with capabilities of being a leader today	% of women with capabilities of being a leader today	Differences in leaders for today (+% favour men,-% favour women	% leadership roles held by men
1	China (Hong Kong)	13.5	13.3	+0.2	67
2	Germany	12.7	14	−1.3	87
3	UK	9.5	11.7	−2.2	80
4	Australia	8.5	12.5	−4.0	76
5	US	8.6	11.8	−3.2	83
6	Switzerland	9.9	9.3	+0.6	78
7	Canada	7.7	9.9	−2.2	75
8	Japan	9.3	6.8	+2.5	95
9	Singapore	9.7	8.0	+1.7	77
10	New Zealand	6.7	9.6	−2.9	72
11	Sweden	7.4	8.2	−0.8	77
12	Taiwan	7.6	6.8	+0.8	73
13	France	6.6	6.4	+0.2	76
14	Thailand	8.2	5.9	+ 2.3	61
15	Finland	6.9	6.7	+ 0.2	73
16	Belgium	6.6	6.2	+ 0.4	79
17	Spain	6.3	6.4	−0.1	76
18	Turkey	5.1	8.3	−3.2	69
19	Italy	5.5	5.5	0.0	64
20	South Africa	4.5	6.8	−2.3	72
21	United Arab Emirates	5.0	6.5	−1.5	85
22	Mexico	5.3	8.0	−2.7	82
23	Denmark	4.5	6.1	−1.6	85
24	Brazil	6.9	5.5	1.4	73
25	Norway	4.5	6.5	2.0	58
	Average	*7.5*	*8.3*	*0 .8*	*76*

- poorer relationships with other team members
- lack of work ethic and motivation
- lacking ambition[9]

As with all groups, it's important to recognize that they are not homogeneous. This applies to disability just as much as to any other group of people and is the point that was powerfully made by Dianna Stone and Adrienne Colella in a thought leadership article which proposed a new model of identifying and dealing with the issues disabled people face in the workplace.[10]

One of the key points they made was that it's not helpful to think of the stereotype of a disabled person. Instead there are stereotypes associated with subtypes of each category of disabled person and these are determined by a number of factors, including:

- the nature of the disability
- aesthetic qualities
- origin
- course
- disruptiveness
- danger or peril
- gender
- race
- status and power

First, the stereotypes will depend on the nature of the disability itself. They identified six categories of disability each having its own stereotypes: physical conditions, mental conditions, sensory impairments, learning disabilities, neurological conditions and addictive disorders.

Aesthetic qualities refers to the extent to which the disability makes others feel uncomfortable or even unsettled by the disabled person's appearance. As mentioned in Chapter 2, this is sometimes referred to as aesthetic anxiety.

Where people are seen as unattractive and ugly they are more likely to be avoided, excluded and kept separate from others. In the workplace, they will be less likely to be involved in team activities, customer-facing roles and, because of these factors, will be less likely to be promoted.

Origin refers to the extent to which the person is seen to be responsible for their disability. For example, imagine two people with the same disability. One of them has had the condition since birth, but the other became disabled as a result of a motorbike accident. The latter individual will be perceived even more negatively than the former because they will be seen to be responsible for their condition. This then translates into generalized assumptions about the person's character such as irresponsibility and recklessness.

When the disability is not in the control of the individual, they will be subject to other stereotypes such as being viewed as courageous and virtuous. The paternalistic attitude towards them will mean that they get treated more leniently and possibly even receive more help. In both cases, neither individual will be seen as having leadership capabilities, but for very different reasons.

Course refers to the permanence of the disability. It's important to appreciate that as we age many of us will be disabled at some point in our lives. Some disabilities are temporary and given a period of rehabilitation we will recover from them, for example a broken leg. Impairments like these have very few consequences on an individual's career. However, people whose disability is permanent and even progressive are viewed more negatively as a potential employee.

Where communication flows are felt to be disrupted because of the person's disability they are more likely to be avoided. Part of the reason for this is that people will feel it makes team processes less effective. Another reason, however, is that people will feel uncomfortable around the individual and will be anxious about how to interact with them.

People with certain disabilities will be viewed as being more dangerous to be around. This could include being HIV positive, but it also includes categories of mental illness. Perceptions of individuals being unstable or dangerous will again mean that they are avoided but also not being given the support they need to continue effectively in their work.

Furthermore, the general view of disabled people as being physically weak is markedly different from the stereotypical view of a leader as strong, energetic and powerful. So, in terms of gender, disabled men will be viewed more negatively than disabled women in the workplace.

Racial minorities with a disability will experience greater discrimination because of their double disadvantage.

Finally, people who are in positions of power and have a disability will be viewed more positively than people with less status. They will be accorded greater respect and admiration. The number of disabled people in very senior positions, however, will be relatively small because of the lack of opportunities earlier in their careers.

Stone and Colella's analysis is fascinating and very helpful. It identifies the ways in which disabled people are both categorized and then treated according to different criteria. It also helps us to see the subtlety with which we apply our biases to disabled people, and how this impacts our decisions.

Other research relating to disability used leader-member exchange theory which looks at the relationships between line managers and their direct reports. One large-scale study of over 1,200 people examined the nature of the relationships where either the line manager or the direct report had a disability.[11] Where the direct report had a disability they were given lower performance ratings by their manager compared to team members who didn't have a disability. Where it was the leader who had the disability they were rated as less effective by their direct reports. Again we are circling back to the fact that the manager with the disability didn't match the prototype of what a leader looks like.

There is also an interaction with the workplace culture. Where organizations have implemented high performance work practices, such as precisely those advocated by talent management practitioners and thought leaders, disabled people are more likely to be stereotyped and their performance more subjectively assessed. They will be viewed in a much more stereotypical fashion and as a consequence of this they will feel a greater sense of anxiety and self-consciousness. They will also feel that they are being unfairly treated, particularly when it comes to an assessment of both the quality and quantity of work produced.[12]

The more inclusive an environment is, the more it creates a buffer for these stereotypes and biased perceptions.[13]

Research that looks at the experiences of disabled people in the workplace has identified three key factors which act as obstacles to progress to more senior positions.[14] First not being given opportunities. In one case an individual, who had become disabled whilst at work, noticed a significant difference in attitudes towards him: 'Whereas before the diagnosis the issue was about realizing potential, after the diagnosis the issue was about "well, you've only got half the capacity, therefore we do not believe there is any potential". It's that black and white.' The participants also wondered whether the work they were doing was considered important to the organization or whether it would remain unnoticed and their contribution unacknowledged. Paternalism was present in the way that they were treated because they felt that colleagues and line managers wanted to protect them from carrying out more challenging work. This would then lead to an evaluation that they did not have the potential to progress and take on more senior roles. As one person stated:

> If you can imagine the parent looking after a child, they don't want to stretch them too far and perhaps they don't praise their child enough but they don't overly criticize them even when perhaps they should do. I don't mean negative criticism, I mean 'you could have done this better', 'where do you think you went wrong', sort of thing, 'how would you do it if it happened again'.

The second obstacle was lack of knowledge, which is a consistent theme that emerges from research on disabled people in the workplace. This meant that accommodations were not being made in order for them to be effective in their role. This meant unrealistic expectations were placed on disabled people which led to greater stress.

Lack of support was the third obstacle both on an organizational and team level: 'There are other colleagues who are not at all helpful, who consider that my capability to do less means more (work) for them, which they don't appreciate... so they don't go out of their way to be helpful'.

Instances of team members not accepting a person with a disability as the leader were also evident, for example: 'I had a team working for me and it went well, but there was one person in the team who really couldn't work for me, she could not work for a disabled person'.

The researchers were also puzzled by some of their findings which showed that individuals appeared to be concerned at one level about the welfare of their colleagues with a disability, but on the other hand did not provide the time, the resources or the support that they needed in order to fulfil their duties. This is consistent with the research on stereotypes of disabled people where people display compassion but also view them as less competent.

As with other minorities and underrepresented groups in organizations, the result of interactions like these with colleagues and managers is for people to self-stigmatize and to view themselves as less skilled and competent than others. They will then feel that they are not suited to taking on more challenging and senior positions in the organization.

LGBTQ+

LGBTQ+ people are constantly aware of the need for safety about whether they can express their true selves. This applies not just to the working environment itself but also to travelling to and from work through cities and towns, particularly when using public transport.[15] The rainbow symbol is now so closely associated with the LGBTQ+ community and its allies that it can evoke strong emotions and discriminatory actions, for example taxi drivers using ride-sharing platforms are more likely to reject a customer if their photograph had a rainbow overlay.[16]

It should come as no surprise therefore that a study found that when applying for jobs, if a candidate stated on their resumé that they had been involved as a volunteer at an LGBTQ+ organization, this would reduce their chances of being shortlisted by 40 per cent compared to somebody whom it could be assumed was heterosexual.[17] The study also highlighted the fact that gay men were less likely to be shortlisted for roles that require qualities such as assertiveness and decisiveness, as these are typically more associated with masculinity and leadership. This type of discrimination has been observed in many countries across the world.

Similar biases in selection processes have been found for lesbian[18] and transgender applicants[19] again in different countries around the world.

The situation for transgender people is markedly worse. 47 per cent of transgender and gender non-conforming people in America reported experiences of not being selected, being fired or not being promoted on the basis of their identity. In a survey of 6,450 transgender respondents conducted in 2011 in the US, 47 per cent reported that they had experienced an adverse job outcome such as being fired, not hired or denied a promotion because of being transgender or gender non-conforming.[20] Similar results have been found in Ireland[21] as well as in the European Union where over a third of transgender people said that they have been discriminated against when looking for a job.[22]

Research has found a significant pay gap between heterosexual and LGBTQ+ people – a gap that starts at the entry level in organizations, which is then exacerbated throughout the rest of their careers.[23] One of the reasons this occurs is that members of the LGBTQ+ community are more likely to be found in female-dominated occupations where pay is typically lower.

10 per cent of LGBTQ+ employees said they had been denied promotion in the previous year because of their identity,[24] something that has been referred to as the gay glass ceiling.[25] Gay men were also rated as less effective leaders.[26]

Harassment and bullying of LGBTQ+ employees is a serious issue they have to contend with. In the UK, LGBTQ+ staff experience bullying and harassment two–three times more than straight colleagues: 6.4 per cent of heterosexual respondents, 13.7 per cent of gay men, 16.9 per cent of lesbians and 19.2 per cent of bisexuals. They were also more likely to experience the stress of not having enough resources and time in order to do their job to the standard required, and have a very similar experience to that of disabled people in the workplace.[27]

International surveys,[28] as well as research in specific countries including the UK[29] and the US,[30] have shown that bullying and harassment is a serious issue for LGBTQ+ people.

Stigmatized individuals can also be excluded or ostracized: not invited to events, not given access to information they need to carry out their work and not communicated with on a regular basis. Here, it isn't actions aimed directly at individuals that exclude them from the team but the withdrawal of resources and relationships. The consequence of this is that LGBTQ+ staff are approximately twice as likely to experience anxiety and depression compared to non-LGBTQ+ colleagues.[31]

There is a consistent finding that gay men are seen as poorer leaders primarily because of the stereotypes associated with them.[32] Lesbians, by contrast, are seen as better leaders than gay men because their stereotypes are more masculine. The reason for this is explained by gender inversion theory, which was first described by psychologists Mary Kite and Kay Deaux in 1987.[33] They identified that gay men and lesbians are viewed very differently, but that the former were more closely associated with the stereotypes around heterosexual women. Lesbians, however, were viewed more like heterosexual men. Part of the reason this has been suggested is because one aspect of masculinity is to be attracted to women. Similarly, being attracted to men is something attributed to femininity. Therefore, with gay men and lesbians the stereotypes become inverted which then enables the qualities of masculinity and femininity to remain intact.

Another major issue faced by LGBTQ+ employees is how open they should be about their sexuality in the workplace. This presents important ethical dilemmas for individuals because they have to be careful how they present themselves in the workplace. There are risks, as this section has shown, in being 'out' at work, with individuals risking experiencing discrimination, bullying and harassment.

Former CEO of BP, John (now Lord) Browne, kept his sexual orientation a secret throughout the whole of his career. In his book *The Glass Closet*, he gives a very honest account of his working life and the struggles he had to maintain this aspect of his identity out of view from his colleagues. Recognized as one of the most talented CEOs of his generation, Browne doubted he could ever have risen as far as he did if he had not remained in the closet. If ever we needed evidence that without examining our biases and prejudices we will never be able to make the most of the talent available to us, surely his experiences provides it.[34]

Race

Research has consistently shown that minorities face considerable discrimination when applying for jobs. This research has been carried out in many countries with the same overall outcome. More recently the results of a large-scale study involving 12,000 job applications was published, although this research had a twist to it.[35] It was looking to see whether the levels of discrimination differed according to the seniority of the role.

In line with the leadership prototype model, the researchers hypothesized that minorities would be considered suitable for more junior positions but would find it difficult to be shortlisted for leadership positions. For the non-leadership roles, over one-fifth (21.2 per cent) of the applicants with English names were shortlisted compared to just over one-tenth (11.6 per cent) of applicants with non-English names. Those with English names were almost twice as likely to be shortlisted even though their qualifications and experience were identical.

As shocking as this is, the results for leadership positions were even worse. The results for the minority applicants being shortlisted dropped slightly to 11.2 per cent whereas the majority-sounding applicants improved their success rate to 26.8 per cent. Minorities therefore, in this study, experienced discrimination for whatever type of role they were applying for, but it was worse for leadership positions. The level of discrimination didn't change if the job required learning, creativity or innovation, but increased if some level of customer contact was needed. The researchers concluded that there is in fact a glass ceiling for minorities who are seeking to move into leadership positions.

Discrimination against minorities for leadership roles is a way of maintaining the status quo, which is to the advantage of white men. This was the conclusion reached by researchers who found that black leaders were rated and viewed less positively by their subordinates than white leaders.[36] Leadership positions are scarce and if competition was increased it would mean that fewer people from the dominant group would be able to obtain them. These may not be deliberate or conscious acts to undervalue those who are underrepresented at senior levels, but the effect is to grant greater access to more senior opportunities to those who are from the dominant group.

When people are given information about a company, but not details about the individuals, they assume that the leaders will be white and that the minorities will be in the lower-ranking positions.[37] The leadership prototype therefore gives white employees a distinct advantage because they are more likely to be seen as a leader than minorities would be.

The leadership prototype involves leaders being assertive and showing dominance. This will be displayed in the language they use and in terms of their non-verbal behaviour.[38] Where a person doesn't fit the prototype the followers are more sceptical and are less inclined to treat the leader with respect. This will be revealed in their body language, which will be more constrained, and they are more likely to undermine the authority of the minority leader by challenging decisions and seeking out second opinions from other white managers in the organization.[39]

When it comes to prototypes for minority groups some surprising effects are found. It's easy to assume that the stereotypes for different ethnic groups are principally describing men from that group. That is likely to be true for white people but not for minorities necessarily. You would think it would be easy to categorize faces according to their ethnicity and gender, for example. This is the case for white men, white women, black men and Asian women. However, we find it harder to categorize black women and Asian men, because racial stereotypes are also gendered. In one study, people were asked to write 700 words about a college senior who was described as either being white, black or Asian without the gender of the individual been specified. When writing about a black college senior they were more likely to be described as male, whereas the Asian was more likely to be described as a female. More research has supported these findings and it has shown that black men and women share the male stereotypes, and Asian men and women share the female stereotypes. This has important implications in terms of the type of jobs people are considered suitable for, particularly when it comes to leadership.

In 2018 I looked at how stereotypes impact the perception of white, black and Asian people in terms of their suitability for leadership roles. I used the Pearn Kandola leadership model for the basis of the analysis. This has three elements of leadership: task leadership, people leadership and thought leadership. Task leadership refers to setting goals, creating plans, monitoring performance and accepting responsibility. Thought leadership relates to technical competence and expertise, innovation, creating a vision and being strategic. People leadership refers to inspiring others, being inclusive and building an effective team.

It's important to bear in mind that the following descriptions are based on the stereotypes of the different groups not their actual characteristics, traits or abilities.

White men are typically considered to be strong on task and thought leadership and weaker on people leadership. White women, on the other hand, are considered to be strong on people leadership but weaker on task and thought leadership. The white male stereotype more closely fits the prototype of a leader than any other group.

They will find it easier to establish relationships with team members and to get respect from them. They are nevertheless weaker on empathy, compassion and caring.

Stereotypically, white women are seen as being stronger in terms of compassion, caring and empathy – precisely those areas where white men are weaker. So, when people talk about the need to have women in a leadership team because they provide complementary qualities to the men, they are only talking about white men and white women. These are the only groups that provide this match, according to the stereotypes.

Stereotypically, Asian men are viewed as strong on thought leadership but weaker on task and people leadership. Asian women are seen in exactly the same way. The prototypical Asian therefore is seen as having female qualities. The stereotypes associated with Asian people include being competent, intelligent, educated, shy, subservient and quiet. Where Asian men and women conform to the stereotype they are likely to be accepted in the workplace. However, when they behave in a way that is counter-stereotypical they are more likely to experience harassment. Being seen as educated and having expertise in a specific area means they are more likely to be in professional roles than general managerial ones. They won't be seen as leadership material in other words.

The stereotypes of black men typically revolve around physicality, strength and athleticism. When it comes to leadership positions none of these things are particularly relevant, and so they will find it harder to be considered suitable for such roles. Black women are stereotypically seen as being stronger on task leadership and getting things done, but not on thought leadership or people leadership. Black women will be respected for their ability to achieve results but heaven help them if they should make a mistake. Consistent with the view that the prototypical black person has masculine characteristics, black women are often described as being aggressive when they display enthusiasm, passion or even scepticism.

The stereotypes associated with minorities have to be overcome if they are ever to be considered to have the potential to be leaders. In looking at the stereotypes, however, we need to recognize that the way that they operate is not the same for all ethnic groups.

It's not necessarily that easy to write these stereotypes down knowing that they will be shared publicly. Nevertheless, it is important that we address these as honestly as we can otherwise we will not change the current position that we face, where there is a dearth of minorities in leadership positions.

Key points

Leadership categorization theory offers a powerful lens for understanding the role of perception, cognitive schemas and social expectations in leadership dynamics. By focusing on the prototypes that followers use to recognize and evaluate leaders, the theory sheds light on why certain individuals emerge as leaders, how leaders are perceived, and how biases and stereotypes can influence leadership outcomes. However, it also raises important questions about the fluidity of leadership and the potential for bias in the leadership selection process. As leadership continues to evolve in an increasingly diverse and dynamic world, recognizing the implications of leadership categorization theory will be essential for developing more inclusive and effective leadership models.

By looking at the experiences in the research on underrepresented groups in leadership we can start to see some of the common themes. First, the stereotypes associated with each of the groups renders them less likely to meet the leadership prototype. This impacts their experience in organizations from the moment they join, to the way their performance is appraised, to their identification as potential leaders of the future.

For those from underrepresented groups at senior levels in organizations, behaving in leader-like ways, by showing confidence, assertiveness and determination, doesn't necessarily bring the rewards that it would do for white men as they are more likely to be disliked.

The members of their team who also hold a leadership prototype will be more likely to withhold their respect and to undermine their authority by challenging decisions and seeking advice from white men people outside of the team.

This will limit their effectiveness as leaders and consequently will prevent them from making further progress in the organization. The lack of mentors, and a viable network, means that they are unable to get the support they need to overcome the challenges that they face.

It is very rare for me to come across people involved in the talent function who are prepared to even discuss these topics, never mind finding ways to address them.

Notes

1   R G Lord, R J Foti and C L De Vader. A test of leadership categorization theory: internal structure, information processing, and leadership perceptions, *Organizational Behavior and Human Performance*, 1984, 34 (3), 343–78

2   K Conger. Exclusive: Here's the full 10-page anti-diversity screed circulating internally at Google [Updated], Gizmodo, 5 August 2017, https://gizmodo.com/exclusive-heres-the-full-10-page-anti-diversity-screed-1797564320 (archived at https://perma.cc/W6QF-EQF7)

3   J Gray (1951/1992) *Men Are from Mars, Women Are from Venus: A practical guide for improving communication and getting what you want in your relationships*, HarperCollins, New York

4   R E Park and E W Burgess (1924) *Introduction to the Science of Sociology*, vol 1, University of Chicago Press, p. 76

5   A H Eagly, S J Karau and M G Makhijani. Gender and the effectiveness of leaders: a meta-analysis, *Psychological Bulletin*, 1995, 117 (1), 125

6   S B Robbins, T A Judge and T T Campbell (2010) *Organizational Behaviour*, Pearson

7   F J Landy and J M Conte (2009) *Work in the 21st Century – An introduction to industrial and organizational psychology*, 3rd edn, John Wiley, New York

8   S A Woods and M A West (2020) *The Psychology of Work and Organizations*, 3rd edn, Cengage

9   J Cunningham, P James and P Dibben. Bridging the gap between rhetoric and reality: line managers and the protection of job security for ill workers in the modern workplace, *British Journal of Management*, 2004, 15 (3), 273–90

10   D L Stone and A Colella. A model of factors affecting the treatment of disabled individuals in organizations, *Academy of Management Review*, 1996, 21 (2), 352–401

11   D J Dwertmann and S A Boehm. Status matters: the asymmetric effects of supervisor–subordinate disability incongruence and climate for inclusion, *Academy of Management Journal*, 2016, 59 (1), 44–64

12   K Hoque, V Wass, N Bacon and M Jones. Are high-performance work practices (HPWPs) enabling or disabling? Exploring the relationship between selected HPWPs and work-related disability disadvantage, *Human Resource Management*, 2018, 57 (2), 499–513

13   D J Dwertmann and S A Boehm. Status matters: the asymmetric effects of supervisor–subordinate disability incongruence and climate for inclusion, *Academy of Management Journal*, 2016, 59 (1), 44–64

14   D Wilson-Kovacs, M K Ryan, S A Haslam and A Rabinovich. 'Just because you can get a wheelchair in the building doesn't necessarily mean that you can still participate': barriers to the career advancement of disabled professionals, *Disability & Society*, 2008, 23 (7), 705–17

15   A Weintrob, L Hansell, M Zebracki, Y Barnard and K Lucas. Queer mobilities: critical LGBTQ perspectives of public transport spaces, *Mobilities*, 2021, 16 (5), 775–91

16   J Mejia and C Parker. When transparency fails: bias and financial incentives in ridesharing platforms. *Management Science*, 2021, 67 (1), 166–84

17   A Tilcsik. Pride and prejudice: employment discrimination against openly gay men in the United States, *The American Journal of Sociology*, 2011, 117 (2), 586–626

18   D Weichselbaumer. Sexual orientation discrimination in hiring, *Labour Economics*, 2003, 10 (6), 2003, 629–42, https://doi.org/10.1016/S0927-5371(03)00074-5 (archived at https://perma.cc/U2EF-CN2T)

19   F Dispenza, L B Watson, Y B Chung and G Brack. Experience of career-related discrimination for female-to-male transgender persons: a qualitative study, *The Career Development Quarterly*, 2012, 60, 65–81

20   J M Grant, L A Mottet, J Tanis, J Harrison, J L Herman and M Keisling (2011) Injustice at Every Turn: A report of the National Transgender Discrimination Survey, National Center for Transgender Equality and National Gay and Lesbian Task Force, Washington

21   J McNeil, L, Bailey, S Ellis and M Regan (2013) *Speaking from the Margins: Trans mental health and wellbeing in Ireland*, Transgender Equality Network Ireland, Dublin

22   European Agency for Fundamental Human Rights (2014) *Being Trans in the European Union: Comparative analysis of EU LGBT data*, https://fra.europa.eu/en/publication/2014/being-trans-eu-comparative-analysis-eu-lgbt-survey-data (archived at https://perma.cc/6YUH-ATK7)

23 M Folch. The LGBTQ+ Gap: recent estimates for young adults in the United States, 1 April 2022, http://dx.doi.org/10.2139/ssrn.4072893 (archived at https://perma.cc/ES62-BD43)

24 C L Bachmann and B Gooch (2018) *LGBT in Britain: Work report*, Stonewall

25 J Frank. Gay glass ceilings, *Economica*, 2006, 73(291), 485–508

26 J W Morton. Think leader, think heterosexual male? The perceived leadership effectiveness of gay male leaders, *Canadian Journal of Administrative Sciences*, 2017, 34 (2), 159–69, https://doi.org/10.1002/cjas.1434 (archived at https://perma.cc/8MH3-SSUW)

27 H Hoel, D Lewis and A Einarsdóttir (2014) The ups and downs of LGBs' workplace experiences, Manchester Business School

28 ILO (2013) Discrimination at work on the basis of sexual orientation and gender identity: results of pilot research, www.ilo.org/resource/conference-paper/gb/319/discrimination-work-basis-sexual-orientation-and-gender-identity-results (archived at https://perma.cc/B6LJ-WN6T)

29 C L Bachmann and B Gooch (2018) *LGBT in Britain: Work report*, Stonewall

30 Williams Institute (2024) LGBT People's Experiences of Workplace Discrimination and Harassment, https://williamsinstitute.law.ucla.edu/wp-content/uploads/Workplace-Discrimination-Aug-2024.pdf (archived at https://perma.cc/H9WS-A5DD)

31 W Dupreé and J Robinson. LGBT experiences; Here's what we know, Gallup, 28 June 2022, www.gallup.com/workplace/393983/lgbt-employee-experiences-know.aspx (archived at https://perma.cc/53CN-69FQ)

32 G Wang, D S Steffensen, P L Perrewé, G R Ferris and S L Jordan. Does leader same-sex sexual orientation matter to leadership effectiveness? A four-study model-testing investigation, *Journal of Business and Psychology*, 2021, 1–24

33 M E Kite and K Deaux. Gender belief systems: homosexuality and the implicit inversion theory, *Psychology of Women Quarterly*, 1987, 11 (1), 83–96

34 J Browne (2014) *The Glass Closet: Why coming out is good for business*, Harper Business

35 M Adamovic and A Leibbrandt. Is there a glass ceiling for ethnic minorities to enter leadership positions? Evidence from a field experiment with over 12,000 job applications, *The Leadership Quarterly*, 2023, 34 (2), 101655

36 S Gündemir, A C Homan, C K De Dreu and M Van Vugt. Think leader, think white? Capturing and weakening an implicit pro-white leadership bias, *PloS One*, 2014, 9 (1), e83915

37 A S Rosette, G J Leonardelli and K W Phillips. The white standard: racial bias in the leader categorisation, *Journal of Applied Psychology*, 2008, 93, 758–77

38 D S De Rue and S Ashford. Who will lead and who will follow? A social process of leadership identity construction in organisations, *Academy of Management Review*, 2010, 35, 627–47

39 S Nkomo. Moving from the letter of the law to the spirit of the law: the challenges of realising the intent of employment equity and affirmative action, *Transformation: Critical Perspectives on Southern Africa*, 2011, 77 (1), 122–35

7

The failings of DEI

Talent management processes and strategy need to be reconsidered, reviewed and revised. The way talent management is designed and then delivered does not adequately identify and develop those who have leadership potential, but instead leads to the continuation of the status quo. Ironically, some of the initiatives undertaken in the name of diversity, equity and inclusion (DEI) don't help to achieve meaningful change either, and may in fact hinder progress towards fairer and more effective organizations.

I want to take a look at two areas of DEI, that are popular yet problematic:

- numerical targets
- affirmative action

Targets

'What gets measured gets done!' is a line that I've been told on a regular basis over the course of my career. This is the principal argument behind the setting of numerical targets or goals to achieve greater diversity by a specific deadline. If the essential components (target number and date) can be forced into an elliptical construction (for example a popular one was 20 per cent by 2020), then all the better. The targets or goals will get the organization some publicity when they are launched and then... well, we won't hear much about them again.

Norway was one of the first countries to introduce mandatory targets for women as non-executive directors. The legislation was passed in 2003 and stated that 40 per cent of non-executive director positions and public liability companies had to be women. The success of this initiative is always given as a reason why targets and goals of this kind are necessary if progress is to be achieved. It's a vindication of the statement 'what gets measured gets done!'. But it does depend on what we mean by 'done'. If it's the achievement of that single goal then without question it has been 'done'. Regularly I will be informed that the achievement of the 40 per cent target in Norway has led to even bigger changes, for example that more women are progressing into leadership roles, that others have been inspired to move into business, etc.

A systematic investigation[1] of the impact of the Norwegian quota system published 16 years after its introduction found a reduction in the pay gap between male and female non-executive directors and more people with children on the boards. Prior to the introduction of the quota scheme it had been argued that there were fewer qualified women than men able to take up such positions and furthermore that fewer women wanted to be in these roles.

Both of these arguments were found to be false – there was no reduction in the qualifications of board members and, when they were approached, women were as keen to take up the roles as men.

An argument that is consistently made about the need to change the make-up of board directors is that this will then have an impact at lower levels in the organization, that more women will be developed for and promoted to senior management positions. Having more women on boards, it's suggested, will mean that they – the women – will advocate for policies such as flexible working and closing the gender pay gap. Furthermore, female board members will suggest more women for senior positions and the boards will be more inclined to select them. A detailed statistical examination of such arguments was undertaken by economist Marianne Bertrand and her colleagues[2] and the conclusion of their analysis was that it 'fails to find much evidence of a positive impact of greater female representation on corporate boards for the outcomes of women employed in these organizations'. They continued: 'In fact, the most robust results in this analysis suggest some possible negative effects on women's representation' (p. 217).

When they looked at the representation of women at senior levels more generally, including organizations who were not affected by the change in legislation, they concluded that 'any improvement in outcomes for women at the very top seem to be concentrated among the women who are directly affected by the reform: that is the women who become board members' (p. 223). The change in legislation, had very little impact, if at all, on the opportunities provided to women in Norway, beyond the women who were promoted onto boards.

Their overall conclusion was:

> When looking for evidence of any such spillovers in the subset of the economy where we would expect them the most, the evidence is more discouraging. We see no evidence of improvements for women working in firms most affected by the reform, suggesting that the new female board members are not significantly changing the opportunities for women within the firm. Additionally, we find no evidence of effects on the set of highly qualified women who would be candidates for board positions, regardless of firm. (p. 228)

So, board membership was 'measured' and got 'done'. That is an achievement that needs to be acknowledged. However, not only did the impact of quotas fail to go beyond that, they may even have had negative effects.

The approach adopted in Norway is sometimes referred to as a legal quota. People will argue that in their organization they don't have such quotas, but they have an aspirational figure. In other words, a target that will be monitored and reported on, but with no date specified for its achievement.

Other organizations have targets with a fixed deadline (e.g. 25 per cent by 2025). Occasionally, figures will be set for more than one group for example minorities as well as women. These are tandem targets, again with or without a specified deadline.

In the UK, there used to be targets for disabled people in employment but that has long since been discarded. I have never come across targets for LGBTQ+, religion, class, refugees or any other dimension. This means that that having targets, in practice, is to achieve greater representation of white women – this isn't a policy to increase diversity beyond this one, albeit important, aspect. Setting more targets than this one is seen by some as diverting attention and energy from this goal.

In 2014 the UK's coalition government launched the 2020 Campaign, the intention of which was to ensure that by 2020 there would no non-executive board of a FTSE 100 company that was all white.

The response to this campaign caught the author and *Times* journalist Satnam Sanghera's attention. One group's response in particular was: 'setting more targets for companies just leads to gridlock and resentment' and that 'the last thing that anyone who wants better boards wants is a "manufactured" board, which is the danger of multiple targets'. The reason this caught Sanghera's attention was that the criticism came from an organization called the 30% Club – dedicated to achieving 30 per cent of women on FTSE 100 boards. Sanghera's anger, whilst controlled, was palpable. He said 'it is strange hearing a pressure group named after a target arguing against targets'. The statement made it quite clear that the interests of the Club lay in advancing the position of white women with no consideration given to the fact that 50 per cent of people from minority groups are female.

This was a continuation of the exclusion of minority women from feminist movements and a failure to recognize their concerns. Attention was drawn to this by the work on intersectionality pioneered by Kimberlé Crenshaw,[3] which showed how issues affecting minority women were ignored by the law and by organizational policies.

It is a great example of the ways in which the concerns of women can be separated from those of minorities, a view summed up by the council member, a white woman, of a Russell Group University who was at a meeting I was also attending. When it was pointed out to her that there seemed to be little attention paid to race issues, her response was: 'Let's work on gender equality first and then move on to race'. This is an attitude that has prevailed for as long as equality for women has been discussed. In 1913, the organizers of the Washington Woman Suffrage Procession were thrown into confusion when black women turned up to what was intended to be an all-white demonstration. The black campaigners were told that they could only join if they went to the back of the procession.[4]

Quotas have long been used in politics to achieve greater representation of women as well as minorities. Detailed research[5] looking at the effects of quotas using data from around the world provides an additional insight into the outcomes achieved. Where there were quotas used by political parties or imposed nationally, majority women benefited the most, and they were of least benefit for minority men. However, minority men benefited from the use of minority quotas. Mixed quotas (a combination of party and national) benefited majority women and minority men. Minority women only benefited from the use of tandem quotas, i.e. for both minorities and women.

Overall, there are winners and losers for each strategy adopted, but in none of the approaches were majority men disadvantaged.

Although focused on political systems, the results were also interpreted for corporate boards as an example of how they may operate in that context:

> If a corporate board has 10 members, setting aside 4 seats for women
> and 2 seats for minorities is unlikely to benefit minority women. At the
> same time, instituting a rule that 40% of members must be women and
> 20% must be members of minority groups is likely to facilitate minority
> women's incorporation, but may, in fact, lead to underrepresentation
> of majority women. A third strategy would be to use nested quotas—
> requiring that women be included among minorities, or that minorities
> be included among women. Such a policy would ensure minority
> women's inclusion without overly displacing other disadvantaged
> groups.' (pp. 14–15)

Quotas and targets, in whatever form, need to be thought about carefully before they are implemented and we need to be aware of the consequences of such policies. Where there are advocates for gender-only targets, and there is total resistance to looking at any aspect of diversity, we should question not only an organization's motives, which are likely to be driven by self-interest, but also the prejudices and biases against other groups. To advocate for targets for one specific group of people, and then to object to this same policy being used to achieve greater diversity for other groups is, at the very least, hypocritical.

Non-executive targets and quota schemes act as a shield and a smokescreen. When an organization is challenged about the diversity of their senior leadership, they can look at the board composition and use this to defend themselves. Gender-based schemes such as these also can hide other inequalities that exist in businesses, and which require a lot more attention if they are to be properly addressed including issues faced by women from the LGBTQ+ community.[6]

Results like this have been known for a long time and I first wrote about my reservations on targets and quotas 30 years ago.[7] A challenge of advocates of such policies put to me is 'How can we achieve change if we don't have targets?' My answer is that I first wrote about this 30 years ago. Targets and quotas are intended to be short-term initiatives, bringing about greater diversity, and yet here we are 30 years later still setting ourselves arbitrary targets in the misguided belief that they will achieve change this time. There has been at least one or possibly two generations that have come into and have left organizations with these policies in place. The impact they have is narrow, and they may hinder opportunities rather than create them.

There are a myriad set of factors that lead to the underrepresentation of women in senior leadership positions.[8] The expectation that setting a target will solve all of these problems quickly is flawed because, first, it doesn't address the complexity of the reasons for underrepresentation, and second, such policies are viewed as being inherently unfair by the majority and others, which then has consequences for the way intended beneficiaries are viewed. Those who such policies are targeted at generally see them in a more positive light, despite the fact that they achieve little in the form of long-term sustainable outcomes.[9]

The stigma of incompetence and the complex
role of affirmative action

Imagine two new joiners have been recruited to your organization, one man and one woman. Both have excellent qualifications and experience. Based on that information alone how would you rate their competence?

Now let me give you a bit more information about the organization and the roles they've been recruited into. The role is a highly technical engineering one and the majority of people carrying out this job are, and always have been, men. Whilst the number of women studying speciality subjects at university have increased over the years, they still represent only 25 per cent of students. The organization has been keen to increase the representation of women in this specialist area and has made it clear that they wish to see a greater proportion of women recruited. Now how would you rate the competence of the two new people?

A study was conducted along these lines 30 years ago by the American psychologist Madeline Heilman. She found that the presence of affirmative action programmes in organizations negatively impacted the assessment of the perceived beneficiaries.[10]

It didn't actually matter whether the job was typically done by men, but if people thought that the person was favoured because of organizational policy, they were seen as being less competent than someone who hadn't benefited from it. Heilman referred to this labelling process as the 'stigma of incompetence'. In addition to white women, black men and black women were also stigmatized in the same way. Her work demonstrated the unintended consequences of affirmative action programmes, which, while well-intentioned, can reinforce biases.

Affirmative action, or positive action as it is referred to in the UK, is a category that covers a wide range of potential actions. The focus in many organizations, at the strategy and policy level, is on those initiatives that bring about changes in the distribution of staff as quickly as possible. The argument is that without providing assistance and support, underrepresented groups will never be able to overcome the barriers that they have faced historically. Attention is typically given to recruitment practices and the setting of hiring goals. Furthermore, line managers may be asked to look at, and where necessary change, the diversity of their teams.

Initiatives like these are intended to increase diversity but problems will be encountered if it is believed by employees in the organization that this at the expense of fairness and objectivity in making decisions about people, seeing it as preferential treatment being given to the underrepresented groups or 'reverse discrimination'.

The result of these perceptions can be seen in Heilman's study, which showed that when a person from an underrepresented group is appointed, against the backdrop of organizational policies designed to address an imbalance in the distribution of staff, they will be seen as the recipient of the assistance that other candidates did not get. The assumption will also be made that had it not been for this extra support, they wouldn't have been appointed. Therefore, the candidates who didn't receive any assistance must've been more competent. As part of the mental gymnastics that are being performed, the person's qualifications and experience will be discounted, so that they are not given the credit that they are due.

For example, a woman in a leadership role at a company with a strong affirmative action policy might find that her colleagues question her qualifications more than they do those of her male counterparts. They might wrongly assume that she was promoted to meet diversity targets rather than because of her skills and experience. This perception can create a hostile work environment where the woman feels under constant pressure to prove her competence, leading to increased stress and decreased job satisfaction.

It also has a damaging effect on the individuals who were the intended beneficiaries. Where they receive assistance and support that they didn't ask for, they will then get an insight into how they are viewed by others. Just think about those occasions when you are perfectly happily undertaking a task, and somebody, unbidden, comes over and gives you some advice, a tip that you might find useful.

I know when this has happened to me, it can arouse feelings of annoyance and a belief that they think I won't be able to complete the task without their assistance. Even brief encounters like this can affect someone's self-esteem and self-confidence, which, as we have seen in earlier chapters, will mean that they won't perform as well as they could.[11] This, in turn, will confirm the views of others, that they are, and always were, less competent than other members of the team. To overcome this perception, they will work harder to prove themselves, which can be exhausting and demoralizing, further entrenching the stigma.

When the person is from an underrepresented group, it can make them question their own capabilities, as well as trying not to conform to the stereotypes that are held about people like them – something known as stereotype threat. People who are the object of affirmative action are also viewed as being of lower status because they are seen as less skilled and competent, and there will be a degree of resentment because they are seen to be competing with others on an unequal and unfair basis. In a meta-analysis of studies looking at the stigma of incompetence, the researchers concluded that it 'is a real world phenomenon with the potential to derail organizational efforts to create and maintain a diverse workforce'.[12] They also found a range of negative outcomes both for the organization and for the objects of the affirmative action programmes. There seems to be enough evidence now that the more forceful the intervention, the less successful it will be both in organizational and individual terms.

A major review of the psychological literature on discrimination conducted in 2017[13] concluded that, in line with other research, there are many contradictions in terms of actions taken and their effects. One damning conclusion they arrived at was that 'efforts to reduce adverse impact and employment discrimination seem to be, at best, moderately effective and, at worst, destructive' (p. 508).

In addition to the findings of the stigma of incompetence and the perceptions that others have of the underrepresented groups, they also noted the impact it has on people's self-esteem, self-efficacy and self-confidence. People can work to overcome the stereotype of being incompetent, but this comes at the risk of being disliked. Furthermore, they also found that mentoring programmes are an effective way of identifying and developing talent, but it only really works if your mentor is white and male. The authors of the 2017 review conclude that 'The complexity of the cognitive and motivational processes underlying bias, and the continuing social, organizational, and political structures, perpetuate such challenges. Ultimately, reduction of bias and adverse impact may require the integration of multiple, complementary theories and strategies that have small independent effects that, when aggregated, achieve sizable change' (p. 508). In other words we shouldn't be looking for the Big Bang or the silver bullet. It's going to be a series of connected smaller actions that bring about change in organizations. It may be good for an organization's public relations to be seen to be taking big, bold actions, which demonstrate their commitment, however, it needs to be recognized that these are not the things that will bring about long-lasting change.

The other option, of course, is to concentrate on those actions that can be taken which make the culture more inclusive. Over time, as people come to understand that it is their behaviour that is creating the blockages, greater diversity at all levels in the organization will be achieved. This takes time and the rate of change may not be in line with some people's aspirations, but often these are unrealistic in any case. I find that in organizations while there is greater resistance to some initiatives and actions, there will be broad support for others (see Figure 7.1).

The following is a list of 12 actions that were presented to the senior executive committee of an engineering firm recently. I asked them which of these they would be happy to carry out:

1 Setting targets for women at senior leadership level.

2 Leaders being prepared to reflect on who they choose to run high-profile projects, and then instead of selecting one of the usual suspects, give someone else a chance to run it.

3 Carrying out an assessment on their own inclusive leadership style and creating a development plan for themselves.

4 Being prepared to give a talk to part of the organization on why DEI is important to them.

FIGURE 7.1 Actions that can be taken

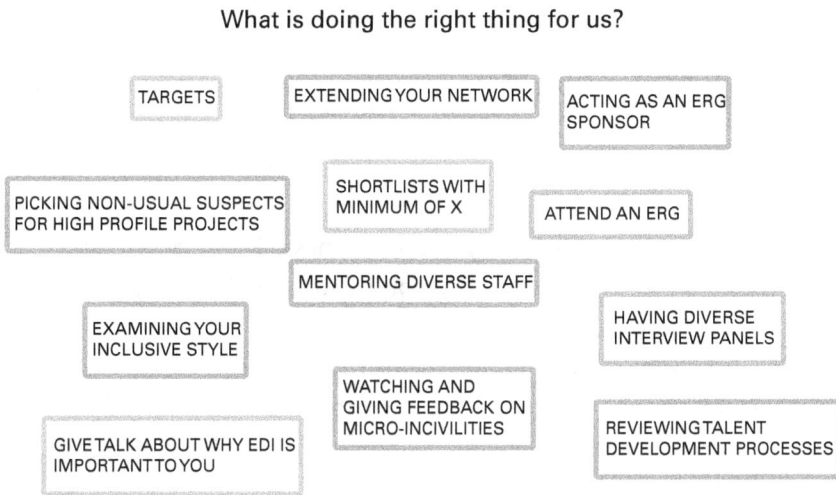

What is doing the right thing for us?

TARGETS	EXTENDING YOUR NETWORK	ACTING AS AN ERG SPONSOR

PICKING NON-USUAL SUSPECTS FOR HIGH PROFILE PROJECTS	SHORTLISTS WITH MINIMUM OF X	ATTEND AN ERG

MENTORING DIVERSE STAFF

EXAMINING YOUR INCLUSIVE STYLE

HAVING DIVERSE INTERVIEW PANELS

WATCHING AND GIVING FEEDBACK ON MICRO-INCIVILITIES

GIVE TALK ABOUT WHY EDI IS IMPORTANT TO YOU

REVIEWING TALENT DEVELOPMENT PROCESSES

5 Carrying out a network analysis to identify the nature of the relationship they have with members of the team and to see who is part of their in group and who are in the out group.

6 For high-profile jobs, insisting that there are at least one or two people from an underrepresented group on the shortlist.

7 Being prepared to act as a mentor for diverse staff.

8 Watching the behaviour of people in their teams and providing feedback on micro-incivilities and other behaviour that could exclude.

9 Being a sponsor for one of the organization's employee resource groups (ERGs). Ensuring that people know that the group exists and seeks to increase attendance at their events.

10 Attending at least one meeting from an ERG – not to give a talk but merely to listen and to learn.

11 Insisting on having a diverse panel of interviewers when selection interviews are being carried out.

12 Carrying out a thorough review of the talent management process to ensure fairness and objectivity.

You can do this exercise yourself. The senior leadership group in question were happy to carry out the vast majority of the actions on the list. There were a couple though that they had difficulty with, in particular setting targets. They were also ambivalent about insisting on the composition of shortlists.

But apart from that, this was a list of actions that they were prepared to commit to. The actions they had the most difficulty with were those which create a sense of inequity and unfairness. They are also the ones that cause the greatest difficulty for members of underrepresented groups. Furthermore, as we have seen, setting targets is problematic in that it never seems to achieve the change that is being sought. Therefore, little would be lost by not engaging in those specific initiatives; and more would be gained by senior leadership undertaking actions that would help to create a culture of inclusion, respect and engagement.

It's easy to conclude that people who object to the more direct and forceful ways of seeking to achieve greater diversity are somehow resistant to change and perhaps have questionable attitudes towards different communities. However, we also have to appreciate that it is only certain actions that people have a strong objection to and these tend to be the ones that seem to contradict the very ideas of fairness and equality.[14]

Professor of Management and Organizations at New York University Stern School of business Lisa Leslie has created a very handy typology of unintended consequences[15] (see Table 7.1).

Initiatives are evaluated on two dimensions: desirable versus undesirable, and the outcome that was affected. There are four types of unintended consequences:

1 Backfire – an undesirable outcome, for example leading to reducing the representation of the target group.

2 Negative spillover where the intended outcome was achieved but with an undesirable effect on non-target groups, for example reducing their representation.

3 False progress where the goal is achieved but there is no real tangible change beyond that, for example extending the levels at which people are considered to be in senior management so that more of the target group are now included.

TABLE 7.1 Typology of unintended consequences of diversity initiatives

	Intended outcome is affected	Unintended outcome is affected
Undesirable effect	Backfire, e.g. reduced representation of target group	Negative spillover – groups other than the target have reduced representation
Desirable effect	False progress – goal appears to be achieved but no real change has occurred, e.g. changing the metrics	Positive spillover – target outcome not achieved but progress in other non-targeted areas, e.g. increase in engagement in other groups

4 Positive spillover where there are beneficial effects but the stated outcome was not achieved, for example, other groups may feel more engaged, leaders may be seen as more inclusive.

It's a useful way of looking at DEI initiatives and provides an analytical tool for practitioners to use to try to predict the consequences of the actions they are about to take. When we look at a commonly implemented initiative such as target setting we can see that it achieved very limited progress towards the target group but has a negative spillover for other underrepresented groups.

Leslie also explains how different initiatives send different signals and these impact the way people respond to them. Where policies are in place that suggest that underrepresented groups are more likely to gain positions, they can send a signal that targeted individuals need help in order to succeed. Where organizations seek to improve the objectivity of their systems for everyone it sends a signal that fairness is valued. It is in these circumstances that positive spillover takes place and where more lasting and sustainable change will occur.

Where organizations seek to win awards and gain external approval for their initiatives it will signal, to the outside world at least, that diversity is valued and that they wish to make progress. PwC, one of the world's biggest accountancy and consultancy organizations, prides itself on the awards it wins for diversity and inclusion. McGregor-Smith's review into race in organizations[16] contained examples of good practice, and it's clear that PwC had the intention of making sure that they were prominently featured. They created a well-publicized campaign designed to address race which they refer to, somewhat coyly, as Colour Brave.

Yet only three years later, the PwC chair, Kevin Ellis (one of whose first acts on taking up the role was to remove the only black partner on the board), was compelled to make a statement in the light of the tragic murder of George Floyd and the Black Lives Matter movement which arose as a result of it. PwC had chosen to put their efforts into marketing and branding, presenting a face to the world that demonstrated their commitment to race equality. The reality was very different and Ellis was forced to run a discussion group with black staff to discuss their experiences, something that he had singularly failed to do in the past. He stated that 'the danger is that when you're uncomfortable is that you shy away from talking', which shows how shallow the Colour Brave campaign was. It also fails to recognize that the key issue here was a determination not to examine the experiences of their black staff previously.

It's a perfect example of what Professor Lisa Leslie is referring to when she talks of 'false progress', where the focus is on awards, accolades and applause but without achieving true change.

Given these challenges, how can organizations implement affirmative action policies in a way that reduces the stigma of incompetence rather than exacerbates it? One approach is to ensure that affirmative action is framed not as a way to give certain groups an unfair advantage, but as a means of ensuring that all candidates are evaluated on a level playing field. This involves making it clear that diversity is valued not just as a social good but because it enhances the organization's overall performance and innovation.

Moreover, transparency is key. When organizations are open about how they make hiring and promotion decisions – focusing on objective criteria and the qualifications of candidates – they can help dispel the myth that DEI leads to the hiring of less-qualified individuals. This transparency can also help build trust within the organization, making it clear that everyone's achievements are valued and respected.

When it is clear that everyone who was hired or admitted met the same rigorous standards, it becomes harder for others to question their competence.

We also need to talk about more things than gender with only a passing reference to other identities. There are numerous ways in which people feel excluded and we fail to acknowledge their experiences in choosing to prioritize those of others above them. In my business, Pearn Kandola, we have carried out research looking at discrimination against people on the grounds of weight, disability, neurodivergence, age, refugee status, religion and class. We have also carried out research when specific events have occurred such as the Covid-19 pandemic, and identified the increases in prejudice against people of Chinese heritage. All of this research has been welcomed by people within those groups because they felt unheard. They have told us about discriminatory behaviour they have experienced and the way that their organizations have responded. Often the organizational response has been to ignore it as if of little interest to them.

Organizations can also take steps to ensure that all employees, regardless of their background, are given the support and opportunities they need to succeed. This includes many of the actions listed earlier which leaders in an engineering company were prepared to sign up to and publicly support. Engaging leaders in this way, which motivates them to make the most of the workforce, is the best way of bringing about change, although it won't happen at the speed that some might wish. But then that level of change isn't possible and trying to achieve it will lead to problems for the underrepresented groups themselves. To ignore over 30 years of research is not just unprofessional, it's plain ignorant.

By creating an environment where everyone is judged based on their contributions rather than their identity, organizations can help to combat the stigma of incompetence.

Key points

Targets, in whatever form they are used, work in a very limited way for the specific group and level that they are focused on. They don't achieve broader change than that and indeed can lead to detrimental effects for other groups who are also underrepresented in their organization. For example, there is a long-standing history of minority women being excluded from initiatives designed to achieve sex equality. It would be interesting to look at your own organization and see whether minority women are truly part of the gender initiatives or whether it is white middle-class women who are the intended targets.

The stigma of incompetence as it relates to affirmative action is a well-documented phenomenon that can undermine the effectiveness of these programmes by leading to negative perceptions of those they aim to help. However, by understanding the roots of this stigma and implementing strategies to counteract it, organizations and educational institutions can better achieve the goals of affirmative action – promoting diversity, equity and inclusion without reinforcing harmful stereotypes.

Organizations are complex and trying to achieve change in an emotional area such as diversity and inclusion is more difficult again. Simplistic solutions to achieve quick results don't work in the long term. Instead we need to look at the whole range of factors that impact a wide range of people in order to bring about long-lasting change.

Notes

1 M Bertrand, S E Black, S Jensen and A Lleras-Muney. Breaking the glass ceiling? The effect of board quotas on female labour market outcomes in Norway, *The Review of Economic Studies*, 2019, 86 (1), 191–239

2 Ibid.

3 K Crenshaw. Women of color at the center: selections from the third national conference on women of color and the law: mapping the margins: intersectionality, identity politics, and violence against women of color, *Stanford Law Review*, 1991, 43 (6), 1241–79

4 K Beck (2021) *White Feminism: From the suffragettes to influencers and who they leave behind*, 1st Atria Books hardcover edn, New York

5 M M Hughes. Intersectionality, quotas, and minority women's political representation worldwide, *American Political Science Review*, 2011, 105 (3), 604–20

6 C P García Johnson and K Otto. Better together: a model for women and LGBTQ equality in the workplace, *Frontiers in Psychology,* 2019, 10, 272, doi:10.3389/fpsyg.2019.00272 (archived at https://perma.cc/ESX5-7GPD)

7 R S Kandola and J Fullerton (1998) *Diversity in Action: Managing the mosaic,* Institute of Personnel and Development

8 R B Adams. Women on boards: the superheroes of tomorrow?, *The Leadership Quarterly,* 2016, 27 (3), 371–86

9 M Coetzee and M Bezuidenhout. The fairness of affirmative action: in the eye of the beholder, *Southern African Business Review,* 2011, 15 (2), 75–96

10 M E Heilman, C J Block and J A Lucas. Presumed incompetent? Stigmatization and affirmative action efforts, *Journal of Applied Psychology,* 1992, 77 (4), 536

11 M E Schneider, B Major, R Luhtanen and J Crocker. Social stigma and the potential costs of assumptive help, *Personality & Social Psychology Bulletin,* 1996, 22 (2), 201–09

12 L M Leslie, D M Mayer and D A Kravitz. The stigma of affirmative action: a stereotyping-based theory and meta-analytic test of the consequences for performance, *Academy of Management Journal,* 2014, 57 (4), 964–89, p. 982

13 A Colella, M Hebl and E King. One hundred years of discrimination research in the *Journal of Applied Psychology*: a sobering synopsis, *Journal of Applied Psychology,* 2017, 102 (3), 500–13

14 C R McCarthy, D S Thomson, S H Barnard and A R Dainty. Pushing the limits: the need for a behavioural approach to equality in civil engineering, *International Journal of Gender, Science and Technology,* 2019, 11 (1), 146–74

15 L M Leslie. Diversity initiative effectiveness: a typological theory of unintended consequences, *The Academy of Management Review,* 2019, 44 (3), 538–63

16 *Race in the workplace: The McGregor-Smith review,* 28 February 2017

8

Developing leaders from underrepresented groups

I have structured the actions that organizations can take to ensure that their talent management processes are genuinely inclusive and its future leaders more diverse under eight headings:

1 Identify your talent management philosophy.

2 Focus on organizational justice.

3 Redefine leadership.

4 Leader behaviour.

5 Mitigate bias.

6 Have the right policies.

7 Use the fairest and most objective tools.

8 Provide support to underrepresented groups.

Identify your talent management philosophy

The talent approach that makes the most noise and gets the most attention is the one that suggests that talent is very rare, it is innate and organizations are involved in a war to attract and retain the most gifted people. Sports are regularly used as metaphors to demonstrate the impact that the most brilliant people have on the success of their teams. Advocates of this approach fiercely adopt and promote the philosophy espoused by McKinsey and its panic-filled report from three decades ago declaring the WFD – War for Talent.

Dr Christina Meyers and Professor Marianne von Woerkom from the University of Tilburg in the Netherlands have shown that whilst this is the most loudly professed approach to managing talent, there are other approaches representing different philosophies[1] (see Figure 8.1). They separate the different approaches on two dimensions: inclusive and exclusive; stable and developable. Exclusive approaches see talent as being very rare; there will be only a small number of people therefore who need to be identified and focused on to ensure that they remain in the organization and are able to function at a high level. Inclusive approaches look at a much broader range of people for development, and whilst they will obviously need to identify future leaders they don't do this by restricting their attention to the ones deemed to be, at a relatively early stage in their careers, the elite.

FIGURE 8.1

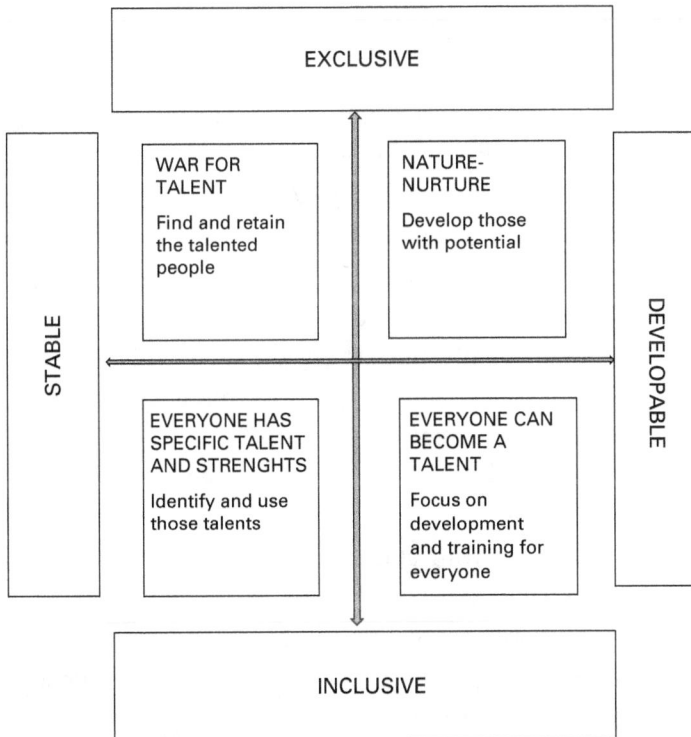

EXCLUSIVE

WAR FOR TALENT

Find and retain the talented people

NATURE-NURTURE

Develop those with potential

STABLE

DEVELOPABLE

EVERYONE HAS SPECIFIC TALENT AND STRENGHTS

Identify and use those talents

EVERYONE CAN BECOME A TALENT

Focus on development and training for everyone

INCLUSIVE

Research looking into the actual practices of organizations shows that there is a split between these two philosophies. The UK's Chartered Institute for Personnel and Development (CIPD), for example, found that whilst most UK organizations, approximately 60 per cent, adopted exclusive processes the others were inclusive.[2]

The second dimension relates to the extent to which talent is seen as a fixed and stable construct or whether it is something that could be developed. If it's stable then the effort will need to go into ensuring that the organization has the most effective tools to identify the people with the necessary qualities. Also considerable effort will go into acquiring talented people from universities and other organizations.

If talent is seen as something that is developable then more effort will go into creating opportunities and experiences for people to stretch themselves and to learn new skills as they progress their careers.

The exclusive and stable approach requires effort to be placed on identifying talented people. Intelligence and personality are key and consequently the tools used will be IQ tests – as they are seen as having high predictive validity – and personality questionnaires. The philosophy advocates the grading of people into A, B, or C players with the greatest amount of resources being given to A players. C players have to be dealt with, typically, by removing them from the organization. For Meyers and van Woerkom this is a 'you either have it or you don't' approach. Efforts will also go into employer branding, promoting the organization as one that is looking for the brightest and the best and, should you be selected, you will be given roles that are strategically important and you will be expected to perform. In return you'll be given opportunities to stretch yourself and the rewards will be great.

An exclusive and developable approach sees talent as potential rather than something that can be identified at an early stage. As Meyers and van Woerkom state, 'Talent is latent: something that is not yet there, but makes certain promises for the future'. Talent is realized through people being developed.

It also accepts that leadership talent is scarce and rather than placing the greatest amount of effort in identifying and rewarding such individuals, there is a balance between identification and development. The person's true abilities will only become apparent through a systematic and efficiently run development programme. This typically has three phases:

1 Separation – identifying people with the potential to move into more senior positions.

2 Transition – providing people with the training and development opportunities to develop their skills and demonstrate their capabilities.

3 Incorporation – taking on more senior positions.

The emphasis here will be on internal employees, giving them opportunities to stretch themselves. But having identified the people with potential to become leaders, they are the ones who will be given the assignments and development to hone their skills further.

Organizations adopting this model will be demonstrating a longer-term commitment to people's development and their careers. They will expect results but they are also expecting people to be learning and adapting based on the challenges faced and the feedback that they receive.

An inclusive and stable approach accepts that everyone has their strengths and that is what we should be focused on. It's inclusive because everyone is being acknowledged in this process, but it's stable because it recognizes that people have strengths and that these differ from person to person. Attention, therefore, is directed towards helping people identify their strengths and then to fit them to the best-suited roles.

The underlying theories for this approach are those that have been developed by the pioneers in this area, most notably Martin Seligman.[3]

The inclusive and stable philosophy also suggests that people do not know what their strengths are, as it's not something they will have considered in much depth before. The talent management process therefore has to help people to gain insight into their own unique strengths profile. The tools that are used will be those that identify people's strengths such as the Values In Action (VIA) Survey of Character Strengths.

People should then be placed in roles that play to their strengths or to adapt their current jobs to suit their profile. Performance management will focus on ensuring the greatest match between strengths and work requirements. Where people are underperforming, a developmental approach will be adopted to continue to develop those strengths and work with someone who has complementary strengths. As a result, people will feel more engaged with their work, their wellbeing will be higher and they will feel happier. They will then feel encouraged to apply their strengths in different areas and in innovative ways.

Organizations that adopt this philosophy are essentially saying that by working for us you will gain a better understanding of what your strengths are, we will apply these to the type of work you do and you will be working in a way that is productive and fulfilling.

The inclusive developable philosophy sees people as having the potential to perform even better than they are currently. Organizations adopting this approach believe that everybody has the potential to do something special. Everyone, therefore, has a special contribution that they can make to an organization's efforts but they also accept that not everyone can be a leader. However, there may be people who have it within them to learn and to grow into leaders given the right opportunities and support. The growth mindset researched and developed by Carol Dweck[4] underpins this approach, as well as Daniel Pink and his work on motivation.[5]

Performance management emphasizes growth and development. Underperformers will obviously have to be managed, and they will be encouraged to learn from their mistakes and to have the confidence to develop their skills further; an approach that will also be applied to those progressing into more senior positions.

The organizational promise in this case is that when you work here you can be assured that you will be developed continuously, and encouraged to learn more about what you are capable of. You will be astonished at what you can achieve with the right combination of challenge, belief and support.

The taxonomy helps us to identify the approaches that are being adopted in organizations and what it means in terms of the processes that are operated that support it, for example performance management and selection methods.

When developing a strategy for talent management it is important that the underlying philosophy is identified, articulated and then communicated. The biggest advantage, however, in having this taxonomy is that it shows we can approach talent management in very different ways, and that the WFT approach represents only one of them. Whichever approach is adopted, however, there can be no excuses for not ensuring that your talent management pool and the leadership are diverse.

Focus on organizational justice

Organizations' approaches to diversity focus on numbers – ensuring that more people from diverse backgrounds are selected into particular roles. As we have seen, one of the most common policies, certainly the one that is most discussed, involves setting targets of one kind or another. Such policies, however, as well as others, have unintended consequences and, ironically, may even lead to less diversity in the future.

Instead I think an approach that focuses on organizational justice will be accepted by a lot more people and, consequently, will create long-term sustainable change. Organizational justice is a concept that revolves around fairness in the workplace. It is crucial in shaping employee perceptions, satisfaction and overall engagement. As organizations strive to foster diversity in their talent management practices, understanding and applying the principles of organizational justice becomes increasingly important.

Organizational justice is generally divided into three main components: distributive justice, procedural justice and interactional justice. Each of these elements plays a critical role in influencing how employees perceive fairness in the workplace.

Distributive justice refers to the perceived fairness of outcomes or distributions within an organization, for example salaries and promotions. Employees evaluate distributive justice by comparing their own treatment, including rewards received, to those of others.

If an employee feels they are being compensated fairly in comparison to their colleagues, they are likely to perceive a high level of distributive justice.

If employees from underrepresented groups feel that these outcomes are biased or unfair, it can lead to dissatisfaction, decreased motivation and, ultimately, to them leaving the organization.

Procedural justice concerns the fairness of the processes that lead to outcomes. While distributive justice focuses on the 'what', procedural justice is more concerned with the 'how'. Employees are more likely to accept an outcome, even if it is unfavourable to them, if they believe the process that led to it was fair. Key aspects of procedural justice include consistency, bias suppression, accuracy, correctability and ethicality.

For talent management, procedural justice is essential when it comes to processes like hiring, promotion and performance evaluations. To achieve greater diversity, organizations must ensure that such processes are designed to be free from bias and are applied consistently across all employee groups. Transparent, well-communicated and consistently applied procedures can help in building trust and promoting a diverse workforce.

Interactional justice deals with the fairness of the interpersonal treatment employees receive from their managers or supervisors and is divided into two sub-components: interpersonal justice and informational justice. Interpersonal justice refers to the degree of respect, dignity and courtesy employees are accorded, while informational justice relates to the adequacy and transparency of the explanations provided to employees regarding decisions and procedures.

Interactional justice is crucial for maintaining a respectful and supportive work environment. Managers who engage in fair and respectful interactions, while also providing clear and honest information, contribute to a culture of inclusion where all employees feel valued and respected. It is important that the experiences of all people are considered and that where team members don't feel included this can be addressed.

Distributive justice will mean ensuring:

- **Equal access to development opportunities:** This will include access to training, mentorship by senior leaders and stretch assignments.

- **Monitoring of opportunities:** Organizations should ensure that we keep track of the opportunities being provided to ensure that they are accessible to everyone, regardless of their background, in order to help build a more diverse leadership pipeline.

Procedural justice will mean ensuring:

- **Bias-free recruitment:** When candidates perceive the recruitment process as fair, they are more likely to trust the organization and feel included from the outset. In the context of talent management, this requires a questioning approach to the services of executive search firms.

- **Transparent promotion criteria:** Organizations should establish clear, objective and transparent criteria for promotion, ensuring that all employees understand what is required to advance. Regular feedback and communication about career development can help employees feel that the promotion process is fair and that they have an equal opportunity to succeed, regardless of their background.

Interactional justice will mean ensuring:

- **Respectful communication:** Interactional justice is key to building a culture where diversity is not just accepted but embraced. Managers should be trained to interact with all employees respectfully and empathetically. This includes being mindful of cultural differences in communication styles and ensuring that all employees feel heard and valued. For instance, encouraging open dialogue and actively listening to diverse perspectives can help foster a sense of belonging.

- **Providing constructive feedback:** Feedback is a critical aspect of talent management, and its delivery can significantly impact perceptions of fairness. Constructive and respectful feedback, when delivered appropriately, can enhance employee development and reinforce a culture of fairness. Too often, people from underrepresented groups are not given timely or constructive feedback.

- **Transparency and information sharing:** When employees feel informed and respected, they are more likely to engage positively with the organization. In group members are more likely to receive information which is helpful and transparent than those in the out group.

In keeping with this organizational justice approach, rather than establishing targets, an organization can have forecasts. They can be created by looking at the distributions of different groups of people at different levels in the organization. So let's say at one level in the organization the numbers of men and women are 50-50. It's anticipated that there will be 10 promotion opportunities during the course of the year, therefore, on the basis of all things being equal, we would reasonably expect that five women and five men would be promoted. Analysis like this could be done for all levels in the organization and so we can see how the diversity at senior levels in the organization will change year-on-year.

I have yet to come across anyone who disagrees with this approach because it is consistent with the overall justice philosophy.

In contrast to the target setting approach, it is not focussed on one or two dimensions and does not create the impression that some groups are being favoured at the expense of others.

Redefine leadership

Organizations will spend a lot of time and effort coming up with a leadership model that applies to their organization. In one organization I was working with they had done great work on whittling down the competency framework for leaders to just five components: motivate, communicate, deploy, engage and execute (descriptions were provided for each of these). When I was asked to comment on them I said that they were essentially looking for a soldier and surely it would be quicker to just say 'we are looking for a bloke'. All credit to the team, they didn't take offence and were happy to put up a spirited defence of those leadership qualities. The point was if they were convinced that this was the model that would work for them, then it was really important that they recognized the ways in which it could replicate bias in the organization, because these qualities are those that are stereotypically associated with white, straight, able-bodied men. If they acknowledged this then it would be part of the means of communicating it to the rest of the organization, alerting people to the importance of these characteristics and what they needed to do to ensure that they were implemented fairly.

In another organization the leadership qualities were summoned up in the acronym JEDI, which stood for judgement, execution, drive and intellect. The senior leaders in the organization would refer to themselves as Jedi. Again I have no particular difficulty with the identification of these qualities, but in referring to themselves as Jedi they were creating a male association. It's something that needed to be discussed when these criteria were being used to assess their staff.

There are many other examples of when organizations have created their competency frameworks and identified qualities such as competitiveness and aggression. If you feel that these qualities are essential then include them by all means. But you need to recognize that these qualities are stereotypically associated with men. Consequently, if people are judged and evaluated in subjective and unprofessional ways, it will lead to bias against groups who, stereotypically, are seen to be lacking in them.

It's a cliché that leadership is about dealing with change. Yet one of the biggest changes that has occurred over the last 40 years is the increasing diversity of the workforce and the impact this has had on organizations. Yet too little attention is paid to leaders being competent to handle this diversity and to create genuinely inclusive organizations. Organizations will have leadership programmes that last months and they might, possibly, have a half-day session on inclusive leadership. This exemplifies to me how inclusion is treated generally speaking: it's an add-on and discretionary.

Inclusive leadership is one of the most essential qualities required to manage the workforce of today and of the future and yet too often is not considered at all. The needs and expectations of the workforce are constantly changing and organizations, and in particular leaders, need to adapt to this. We are currently at an inflection point.

The world has changed, but management theory and management have not. There will be a turning point at which management and management theorists will recognize that the way things are done needs to change. It was just such a moment of change when in 1973 Charles Perrow referred to the dark side and light side of management theory.[6] The dark side represents the status quo, a continuation of the way that we have always done things. The light side represents the new management agenda, the response to the changes that have taken place. Too many of the talent management theorists have taken their starting point as McKinsey's War for Talent report, which failed to take into account the increasing diversity of society, the workforce and employees in organizations. WFT had the effect, if not the intent, of ignoring diversity and ensuring that white, straight, able-bodied men continued to occupy the most senior roles in organizations.

As well as increased diversity, the other change that has occurred is the heightened emphasis on employee engagement and wellbeing. This change was happening before 2020, but the impact of Covid-19 has accelerated it. It is clear from the CIPD's 2023 survey[7] that this, as well as DEI, has been propelled to the top of many organizations' agendas, as the quotes from the report reveals (see box).

'EDI is coming to the forefront of the profession – we are being asked to embed it into all areas of HR'

'CSR and EDI are taking prominence over traditional HR functions'

'HR has become more socially aware than ever to include diversity conditions'

'Employees will demand more visibility on things like corporate responsibility, and expect to have a greater hand in shaping their workplace, and how it operates'

'Engagement is paramount, and L&D is a huge area of focus, especially as the younger workforce demands more from roles'

'We are focusing more on people's well-being, but are mindful of costs. Mental health has become a much bigger topic and HR is leading on how to manage this'

'Employment is much more fluid now, so a different approach to staff, retention and hiring is required'

Research has shown that over the last 100 years each new generation in the workplace is more inclusive than the previous one, and that trend is continuing around the world. Having a talent strategy based on the thoughts of a report nearly 30 years old, with all of the changes that have taken place in the world since then, is misguided.

HR functions are seeing the links between wellbeing, flexible working, EDI and sustainability.

They also recognize that today's younger workforce expects organizations to be paying attention to these issues, and they expect to be treated on their merits.

Having a strategy that achieves the result of more white men in senior positions is not something that will remain credible. It is essential, therefore, that organizations not only incorporate inclusion into leadership profiles and development programmes but ensure that leaders understand the benefit they will gain by creating an inclusive culture.

Leaders also need to be prepared to look at their own behaviour and to lead by example. Leaders should demonstrate a commitment to organizational justice by making fair and equitable decisions, being transparent about those decisions and treating all employees with respect. This sets a tone for the entire organization and influences the organizational culture.

Leaders can also promote organizational justice and diversity by investing in training and development programmes. This includes training on unconscious bias and inclusive leadership. Such programmes help leaders and managers understand the importance of fairness in decision making and equip them with the tools to implement these principles effectively.

Ultimately, they need to ensure that organizational justice is monitored and reviewed by establishing systems and processes. Regular audits, employee surveys and diversity metrics can provide insights into how well the organization is adhering to its commitments. Leaders should be open to feedback and willing to make changes where necessary to improve fairness and inclusivity.

Leader behaviour

Leaders can increase inclusion and reduce bias by placing emphasis on workplace interactions and dynamics between team members.

At Pearn Kandola, we have been working in the area of inclusive leadership since 1999. We have gathered an enormous amount of data since then which we have analysed on a number of occasions. The latest analysis of the data of over 1,000 leaders revealed a number of strengths overall, particularly in the area of creating psychologically safe environments where people feel that they can speak up. This is obviously a critical factor in inclusion so that individuals can be more authentic in the workplace. The areas where leaders needed to do better, however, were recognizing their biases, taking action to mitigate these and addressing in groups and out groups within the teams.

One of the biggest biases that exists is known as an egocentric or self-serving bias. It's where we believe we are better than other people at something, possibly even most things. Most drivers in the UK, for example, believe that they are above average at driving. In an inclusive leadership development programme I was running within a global bank, I posed a question to the 200 leaders who were attending: 'On inclusive leadership, when you compare yourself to your colleagues, do you think you are a) below average, b) average or c) above average?'

What percentage do you think answered above average? The answer is 100 per cent! This was a highly numerate group of people and on seeing the results they laughed. The purpose of our programmes is to enable people to appreciate their strengths when it comes to inclusion and to build on those. It also helps them recognize the areas where they may have blind spots and where they can take action to make their teams even more inclusive.

General sessions, which talk about inclusion and bias, are fine, but when people are given individual, tailored feedback, providing action they can take, there are much higher levels of engagement and motivation. It's not punishing people for not getting things wrong; instead, it's using the work of Daniel Pink, Carol Dweck and Martin Seligman to create an environment where people feel encouraged to try new things out, to make mistakes, to learn and to develop.

Leaders should also be shown how to carry out their own network analysis – how to examine the relationships they have within their own teams, who is in the in group and who is in the out group. The tools are simple and powerful. In our experience we find that increasingly leaders are prepared to engage in this type of self-reflection, in order to create better relationships and enhanced team performance. We need to understand that as inclusive as we may be, the younger generations entering the workplace are more inclusive again. This can cause anxiety among some leaders. Increasingly I have found, because of the impact of social media, that some leaders are nervous about talking about DEI matters within their organization. They are aware of the benefits of speaking about DEI but they have also seen the embarrassment caused to leaders and their organizations when they have used an outmoded expression, for example.

In these situations, it's important that leaders are authentic and prepared to be vulnerable. They should make it clear that their intention in speaking is because they take DEI seriously. Furthermore, it's not their intention to cause offence or to make people feel undervalued – quite the opposite in fact – but should this happen then the feedback would be listened to.

Leaders who I have coached to adopt this approach have actually found it worked extremely well for them and was appreciated by staff in their organizations.

In an earlier chapter, I described the types of micro-incivilities that impact the working lives of women, minorities, LGBTQ+ people and disabled people. These behaviours are indeed micro, but they can be observed. As a leader, you can sit back and observe the interactions of your team members. Who is invited to speak? Who gets inter-rupted? Whose ideas are built on? Whose ideas are ignored? Who is the individual that, when they speak, the others start to roll their eyes? Which people are referred to by name and others not? All of these things and more, including eye contact, have an impact on indi-viduals when they occur on a regular basis. They send a signal to those individuals that they are not valued in this team and that they don't belong. Having seen any behaviours like this, feedback can be given. In many instances, people may not have been aware that this was happening. Therefore, the feedback helps them to change their behaviour to create a more inclusive team environment. (Incidentally, I'm not a big fan of 'calling out' behaviours that may exclude. 'Calling out' suggests that this is done in public and that it involves naming and shaming, but shame is never a good way to try to persuade people to change. There is more than one way of enabling people to change their behaviour to be more inclusive.)

In addition to looking out for micro-incivilities, we can practice micro-affirmations, where we actively seek to adopt behaviours which are welcoming, supportive and inclusive. This helps to create a team environment where people are willing to speak up, contribute their ideas, critique other people's ideas and to value each other's company.

We should also remember that the most significant way to improve our wellbeing, and to increase our lifespans, is the relationships we have with other people. Our personal wellbeing is enhanced by positive relationships with others. As work takes up so much of our lives, the impact of creating a more inclusive environment will be seen in terms of people's overall health and wellbeing.

Finally, leaders should understand that achieving greater diversity in senior levels is not going to happen by taking short-term actions alone. Asking executive search firms to get diverse candidate slates and setting numerical targets on gender may send a signal of intent, but they will achieve very little. As the research shows, they may in fact cause damage. So when looking at initiatives, such as these and others, always consider what the unintended consequences may be.

Mitigate bias

A large part of this book has been showing how our systems for identifying and developing talent are inherently biased. The main reason this happens is because the talent management theorists, academics and some practitioners who endorse the stable and exclusive philosophy show very little concern for issues to do with diversity and inclusion. Consequently, the processes they operate are being judged solely on the succession of leaders that they produce with little regard to whether this has been done, fairly and accurately. If there are groups of people within our organizations who are consistently overlooked for leadership positions, and who are not even considered to have the potential for such positions, how can we possibly say that our systems and processes are effective?

I have taken four groups of people who are underrepresented at senior levels in organizations – women, people with disabilities, LGBTQ+ people and minorities – and shown how bias operates against them. The outcomes are the same, in that they are not considered to have the potential to be leaders, but the mechanisms by which these conclusions are arrived at are different. The stereotypes that exist about each of these groups are compared against the notion that we have of a leader in our heads – the leadership prototype. The leadership prototype fits more closely the stereotypes of white, able-bodied, straight men than any other group.

Therefore, anyone involved in the talent management process needs to be aware of the stereotypes that exist of different groups, the way they can impact our decisions and the need to guard against them.

Some of the biases that have been discussed in the book include:

- The stereotype that women are much better at relationships than directing and leading.

- Stereotypes about LGBTQ+ people vary according to each group but show that they are different from 'normal' people.

- Stereotypes about racial minorities, again, vary according to the group being looked at. Nevertheless, no minority group is seen to be capable of being a good leader, according to the stereotypes.

- Stereotypes about disabled people suggest they can't be good leaders because they are weak, unhealthy and require too many resources.

- Each of these groups experience excessive scrutiny. They have a magnifying glass applied to them, which means that any mistake they make will be blown out of all proportion and damage chances of progression.

- Mistakes and errors in each of these groups will be taken as an indication of general ability. When they achieve success it will be because of special circumstances, such as having a great team or being lucky.

- By way of contrast, in group members will be shown excessive leniency. Mistakes will be forgiven and possibly overlooked. Furthermore, errors will be seen as caused by other factors outside of the individual's control.

- In group members successes will be seen to show something about their inherent superior qualities and characteristics.

- When out groups are being considered for a role in which they are underrepresented, they will have to overcome a higher hurdle than for in group members, something known as shifting standards. In jobs where they are not underrepresented, the barrier for them will be lower, thus there is encouragement and a reward for them to go into areas where they are already present.

- Long hours, total commitment to the job and visibility in the workplace are all seen as positive indicators that someone is making a positive contribution. Attitudes like this, however, show gender, race and disability bias.[8] Furthermore, they show a lack of knowledge about the impact that hybrid working has in terms of improving people's engagement, wellbeing and productivity. This is another major change in attitude that organizations will have to adapt to in order to keep their employees.

Just to reiterate, these are stereotypes and not facts. Research has shown, for example, that disabled people thrive in high-performance working environments, counter to the stereotype attached to them.

Countering bias is not as difficult as it sounds. First of all we need to show people how bias operates in the working environment and in the processes that they are using. For example we have carried out a review within one organization looking at their talent management processes. We conducted a review of the performance appraisal reports that had been written and, in addition, watched moderation meetings being carried out, where managers were discussing the ratings that they had awarded their staff.

The report we produced showed the organization what they were doing well, and what they could improve in order to ensure a fair and robust process. This was carried out in 2019, and the idea was it would be repeated on an annual basis. Of course, events intervened, and this was repeated in 2023. It was heartening to see that the biases evident the first time had reduced even with a lapse of four years. Some biases had crept back into the process, which showed the value of doing the exercise again. This can only happen, though, when you have a leadership team and a talent management organization that is prepared to reflect on their behaviours and their decision making in order to identify those people who have the potential to make much bigger contributions to their organization. The other point to make is that this was designed to encourage people to approach the topic of bias in an open and thoughtful way, not to make them feel ashamed and blamed. The emphasis on the business case for diversity and inclusion has been made elsewhere by other authors, but we should not forget that people respond well to recognizing the importance of fair treatment.

Diversity and inclusion is often labelled as 'politically correct' or 'woke' as if this is purely an identity-driven approach with little concern for an organization's effectiveness and profitability. I don't see it like that at all. By ensuring that we treat people fairly, and that we have assessment methods that genuinely identify people with potential, we increase competition and make our organizations stronger as a result. Of course, if you think that white, straight, able-bodied men are the only ones who can be great leaders, then any challenge to that will be seen as threatening.

Have the right policies

In order for people to demonstrate their true capabilities, we need to have organizations which value inclusion. Organizations such as these enable individuals to feel comfortable in the workplace, show their true capabilities and perform at their best. As we have seen, underrepresented groups experience many forms of exclusion and discrimination, some of which are blatant and ugly (being physically and verbally abused), and many others that are subtle (having ideas ignored, no eye contact, being misgendered or being infantilized). This makes people feel excluded, unsafe and wary in their work-places. This is an extra stress placed upon them, referred to as minority stress, which ultimately impacts their performance.

So the policies that need to be in place are not just those around talent management and DEI, but also policies around bullying and harassment. All of the groups that I have focused on in the book experience high levels of bullying, discrimination and exclusion, all of which will impact their work. If these policies aren't effectively implemented, people from these groups will feel uncomfortable in the roles that they are carrying out.

For those individuals who have an identity that is not visible to others, for example, LGBTQ+ or a non-visible disability, they may choose to keep this hidden from their colleagues in the workplace. This in turn creates extra pressures on them to monitor what they are saying, and who they are saying it to just in case they should reveal this identity.

If you have rarely been in a minority in the workplace you won't be aware of the additional pressures that they experience.

So as well as having the policies and procedures, it's also important for all of us to try and empathize with how our colleagues may be feeling. The technique of perspective-taking is particularly helpful here, where all you have to do is to try and imagine what another person might be thinking, feeling and seeing. We can engage in conversation with individuals and ask questions to see how accurate our perception was. It's important that we suspend judgement in listening to what people are telling us and that we convey empathy.

Listening to feedback from employee resource groups (ERGs) is another way in which we can develop our understanding of the issues faced by particular groups in the organization.

Listening and showing that we are trying to make the workplace more inclusive helps to make people feel comfortable, respected and valued. And all of this feeds into your talent management process, which is something that it is important not to forget.

Use the fairest and most effective assessment methods

The way we go about assessing talent is actually very important. There are a wide variety of methods that can be chosen from which provide measures of, for example, abilities, interests and personality traits.

Standardization is an important feature of a selection test because it ensures consistency in treatment and reliability. Candidates sitting the test will take them in much the same conditions with the same amount of time given to them. There are talent management theorists and thought leaders who recommend the use of intelligence tests because this is linked to success of leaders.

There is, however, surprisingly little consideration given to the adverse impact of such tests, instead what is focused on is their validity. In other words, the argument goes, these tests must be used because they identify the people who will be successful in the future. Yet on the other hand, studies have repeatedly shown that minorities do less well on such tests.

So we are left with something of a conundrum: intelligence tests are predictive of who will be successful as future leaders, and minorities do less well on them. Is it a conundrum though or just an unfinished sentence? Let's try finishing the sentence off: Intelligence tests are predictive of who will be successful as future leaders and minorities do less well on them which means that they (the minorities) are less intelligent. Surely that's what we are being told and if so it's a return to the race-based theories that dominated the 18th and 19th centuries, as well as a large part of the 20th century. It's a thoroughly complacent approach to ignore these considerations completely.

The most effective way of identifying potential in organizations is to use standardized interviews and as realistic assessment methods as possible, so that people can demonstrate their abilities in something that they can identify with. Multi-method approaches such as development centres have proven to be highly effective ways of assessing somebody's current level of skills and capabilities. They can also help to identify their strengths, which they can then build on, and to find ways of developing their areas of relative weakness.

The detailed level of information that can be obtained can also enable people to find the work that is going to be most suited to personality, interests and strengths. It's an ideal way of combining the work of Seligmann, Dweck and Pink to create a supportive and challenging learning environment, where people are able to demonstrate their true potential

The other common practice initiative undertaken by organizations is to create interview panels that are diverse. For some reason this is believed to be a way of increasing the fairness of interviewing. Nobody ever says it, but I suspect the reason behind this is there's an assumption that representatives of different groups of people will have different biases. So a panel of two men and two women would be seen as good because the bias of the men would be cancelled out by the bias of the women and so we will end up with a fair outcome – let's just not be too concerned about how that was achieved.

Research has consistently shown that the most effective way of achieving validity and fairness in interviews is to provide training to the panel members and to have a clear structure that they will follow. Trained interviewers will make better and fairer decisions regardless of the composition of the panel. An untrained diverse panel will make biased and ineffective decisions. For example, we know that full leadership positions have a bias towards men. We also know, and we've known this for a long time, that for leadership positions, women also have a bias towards men. The solution is to train the panel, not to take the easy step of getting a diverse group of people together and expecting them, without any guidance or training whatsoever, to do a half competent job.

Too often, lazy thinking like this, which is not backed up by evidence, sends a tokenistic signal that the organization is taking things seriously, but in fact can't be bothered to make the investments necessary to enable individuals to undertake effectively the task that has been delegated to them.

Provide support to underrepresented groups

Successful leaders achieve because of their inherent qualities, personality and intellect. If people need to have support, special assistance and attention, by definition they are not leadership material. This is all part of the leadership mythology that's been created by the followers of the WFT creed.

It's a myth, because all of those people who have succeeded had support from other people, most notably their mentors and sponsors, and they were allowed to fail, and given time to learn from their mistakes. They had a network, which they could turn to, which would even have stepped forward to assist them without having to be asked.

Yet when we say that these same support mechanisms should be provided for people from underrepresented groups – those that have been covered in this book, women, LGBTQ+ people, ethnic minorities and disabled people – we are then told that this is unfair and that if they need this additional assistance they can't have what it takes to succeed.

It's a ridiculous notion, and if we want to have a more diverse leadership, full of talented people who are able to compete and bring success to their organizations, then we need to be able to create support mechanisms for the underrepresented groups, which will enable them to show their full potential.

In the work we have carried out on inclusive leadership, one of the areas which the leaders themselves identify as something they could do more of is to mentor people who are different to them. It's important not to specify what type of person this should be, because the leaders need to be engaged and motivated to help this person develop and grow. In one German engineering organization I was working with recently, many of the leaders I met with took it upon themselves to talk to those team members they had less contact with to discuss their development needs. This was a conversation that had very rarely, if ever, taken place with these individuals before. One member of the executive board spent an hour with a female executive, listening to her experiences in the organization. He learned a lot from the conversation, and I later heard from the female executive how much she enjoyed the conversation and how much more appreciated she felt after it.

It just goes to show that being mindful about these things can have a lot of benefits both to the individual leader and also to the more junior team members as well. It creates a sense of inclusion and greater confidence in the leader as well.

It's critically important to ensure that when people from underrepresented groups are first appointed to a role, either through promotion or external selection, a close eye is kept on them for the first three to six months. Research has shown[9] this to be the most critical period determining how settled someone will feel in their role.

Preparing an individual for promotion is also an important aspect to be considered. People from underrepresented groups are more likely to experience something referred to as the imposter phenomenon – the feeling that they really don't deserve to have that position or role. Showing them what the job will entail before they start the new role helps to prepare them for the very first few days and reduces the amount of uncertainty that they will experience. This in turn will help them feel less like an imposter. Providing them with a coach to support them through this period or somebody more senior who they can buddy up with will also provide a safe resource for them to call upon when they experience bumps in the road. Table 8.1 provides a list of the signs that a coach or a mentor can be watching out for that will indicate that someone is experiencing the impostor phenomenon.

TABLE 8.1 Signs that someone is experiencing imposter phenomenon

Self-doubt	Frequently questioning their abilities or feeling inadequate despite evident accomplishments
Discounting success	Attributing achievements to luck, external factors or the help of others rather than their own skills or hard work
Fear of exposure	A persistent fear of being 'found out' or exposed as a fraud, leading to anxiety about future performance

(continued)

TABLE 8.1 (Continued)

Perfectionism	Setting unrealistically high standards for themselves and feeling like a failure if they don't meet them
Overworking	Compensating for perceived inadequacies by working excessively or feeling compelled to prove themselves
Avoiding challenges	Reluctance to take on new responsibilities or challenges due to fear of failure or inadequacy
Comparative thinking	Constantly comparing themselves to peers and feeling inferior, especially in professional or academic settings
Minimizing praise	Dismissing or downplaying compliments or positive feedback, often feeling undeserving of praise
Difficulty internalizing success	Struggling to accept accomplishments as a reflection of their abilities, often thinking they will not replicate success
Coping mechanisms	Developing unhealthy coping strategies, such as procrastination or avoidance, to deal with feelings of inadequacy or anxiety

The societal biases have an impact on the individuals themselves because they internalize the stigma. Known variously as internalized sexism, internalized racism, internalized homophobia and internalized ableism, it has an impact on people's self-esteem, self-confidence and self-efficacy. This means that there is a greater chance that people from those groups will feel that they are not capable enough of holding down senior roles, and consequently won't apply for them. They will be more likely to turn down opportunities to stretch themselves by not taking on important, high-profile projects. The majority of this book has been concentrating on the biases that we have towards people from those groups but we also need to be aware of the biases that people hold about themselves. If this isn't tackled and addressed, it means that people will be holding themselves back. Creating programmes where these sorts of topics can be discussed and where individuals from these groups can learn about these phenomena is important. An approach like this shouldn't be mistaken for what is referred to as 'fixing the person', i.e. the implication being that all that is needed is to correct some skill or character deficiency in the person. (In the past, for example, it was not that unusual for organizations to set up assertiveness training for women. The issue actually isn't that women are not assertive, it's that when they are assertive, there is a backlash.) However, in this instance, we are talking about an internal blocker that could prevent individuals from taking up opportunities, even though they have all the skills necessary to do it.

Making an offer to be a mentor rather than waiting to be asked is also important. It is also important that people feel that they also have a sponsor, someone who will recommend them for more senior and challenging roles in the organization. Sponsors have credibility in the organization and recommendations that they make will be given careful consideration. Individuals from diverse backgrounds who are underrepresented will feel hesitant to approach somebody more senior and different to them. Having somebody that they can turn to for advice and guidance is a valuable resource that is often unavailable to such individuals. Furthermore, it's also been shown that people from these groups aren't necessarily aware of the benefits that can be gained by having a mentor and a sponsor.

Concluding remarks

For far too long, talent management has been dominated by an elitist mindset that disregards diversity and inclusion, perpetuating cycles of bias, favouritism and discrimination. This narrow view has allowed the exclusion of underrepresented groups at senior levels and within high-potential talent pools, fostering environments where discrimination and prejudice thrive. In the corridors of power, where talent management holds a special status, some individuals see themselves as detached from the broader HR and DEI initiatives. These are often the same people who resist change, clinging to outdated notions of meritocracy that favour a select few.

For decades, certain management theorists have championed elitism, arguing that leadership potential is the birthright of an exceptional few. In doing so, they have ignored the groundbreaking work of psychologists like Martin Seligman, Carol Dweck and Daniel Pink, who have shown that potential is not fixed but nurtured. They've dismissed the insights of authors like Malcolm Gladwell and Matthew Syed, who've demonstrated that success is often the result of unseen support and opportunity, not innate superiority. The time has come to reject this outdated model and embrace a more inclusive approach to talent management – one that recognizes the potential in everyone, not just those who fit a narrow mould.

The discovery of the entirely fictitious Mountains of Kong led to the belief that there were riches to be found there. Believing in the false promise of gold, colonizers extended their reach into Africa, profiting at the expense of its people. Similarly, the myth of the War for Talent and the construct of talent management has served to justify exclusionary practices that harm not just the individuals left behind but also the very organizations that seek to thrive in a competitive world. The time for change is now. Those involved in talent management have been ill-served by the thought leaders in the field, who have promoted ideas that have long passed their sell by date. The future belongs to those who dare to create a system that is fair, inclusive and truly reflective of the diverse talent that exists within our society. It's time to dismantle the established ways and systems, to rethink how talent is developed and build a new, equitable approach to nurturing leadership. If those who hold these positions cannot adapt, they must step aside for those who will.

Notes

1   M C Meyers and M Van Woerkom. The influence of underlying philosophies on talent management: theory, implications for practice, and research agenda, *Journal of World Business*, 2014, 49 (2), 192–203

2   CIPD (2012) Learning and talent development 2012, www.portfolio-info.co.uk/wp-content/uploads/2024/03/2012-CIPD-Learning-Talent-Survey-Report1.pdf (archived at https://perma.cc/3KEP-3C9S)

3   M E Seligman (2012) *Positive Psychology in Practice*, John Wiley & Sons

4   C S Dweck (2006) *Mindset: The new psychology of success*, Random House

5   D H Pink (2011) *Drive*, Canongate Books

6   C Perrow. The short and glorious history of organisational theory, *Organisational Dynamics*, 1973, 2 (1), 3–15

7   CIPD (2023) People Profession 2023: International survey report, www.cipd.org/uk/knowledge/reports/people-profession-survey- 2023/#:~:text–Upskilling%20and%20developing%20current%20talent,challenges%20or%20areas%20of%20concern (archived at https://perma.cc/Z8JB-X3F6)

8 J M Amis, J Mair and K A Munir. The organisational reproduction of inequality, *Academy of Management Annals*, 2020, 14 (1), 195–230

9 J Hogan, R Hogan and R B Kaiser (2011) Management derailment. In S Zedeck (ed), *APA Handbook of Industrial and Organizational Psychology*, vol 3, *Maintaining, Expanding, and Contracting the Organization*, pp. 555–75, American Psychological Association, https://doi.org/10.1037/12171-015 (archived at https://perma.cc/7383-CMQK)

INDEX

Looking for another book?

Explore our award-winning books from global business experts in Human Resources, Learning and Development

Scan the code to browse

www.koganpage.com/hr-learning-development

More from Kogan Page

From 4 December 2025 the EU Responsible Person (GPSR) is:
eucomply oÜ, Pärnu mnt. 139b – 14, 11317 Tallinn, Estonia
www.eucompliancepartner.com

www.ingramcontent.com/pod-product-compliance
Lightning Source LLC
Chambersburg PA
CBHW060931220326
41597CB00020BA/3495

9 781398 618084